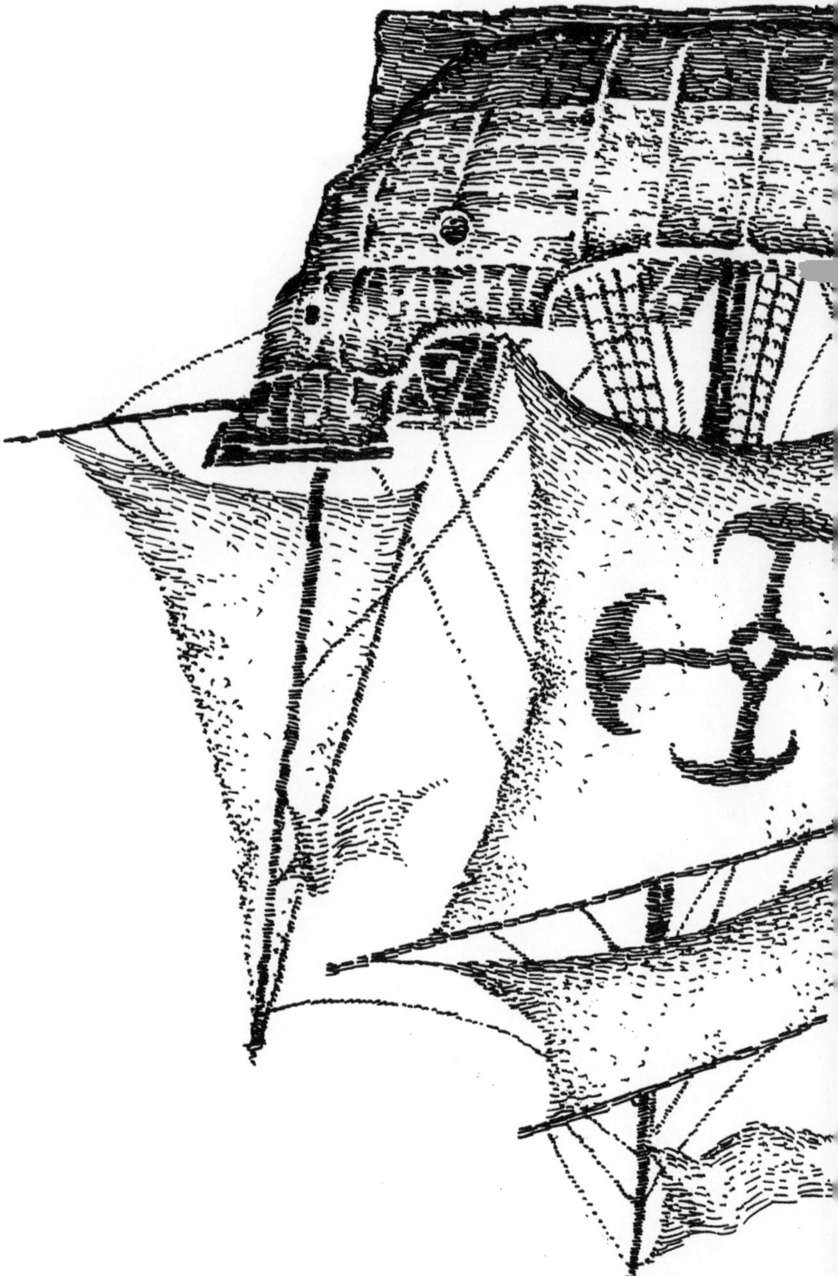

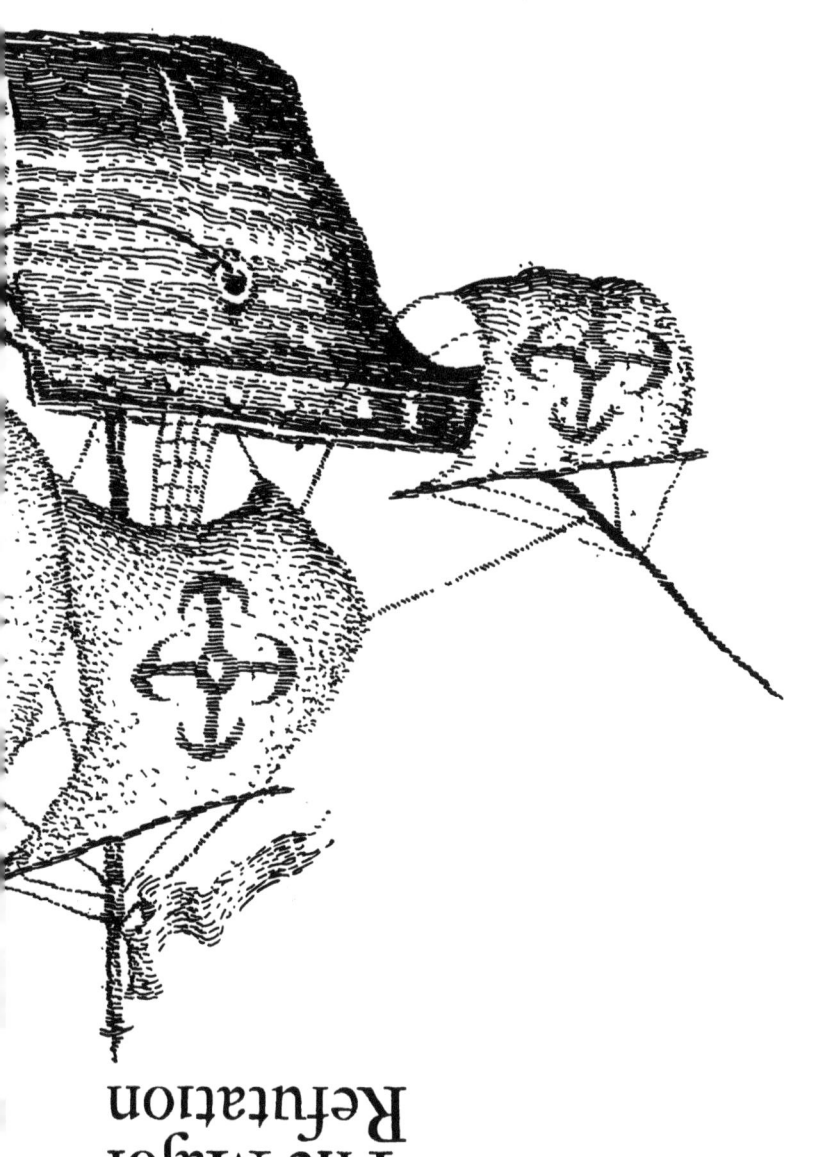

The Major Refutation

Pierre Senges

The Major Refutation

English version
of *Refutatio major,*
attributed to Antonio de Guevara
(1480 – 1545)

Translated by Jacob Siefring

Contra Mundum Press   New York · London · Melbourne

Translation © 2016 Jacob Siefring; *La réfutation majeure* © Editions GALLIMARD, Paris, 2005.

First Contra Mundum Press Edition 2016.

All Rights Reserved under International & Pan-American Copyright Conventions. No part of this book may be reproduced in any form or by any electronic means, including information storage and retrieval systems, without permission in writing from the publisher, except by a reviewer who may quote brief passages in a review.

Library of Congress Cataloguing-in-Publication Data

Senges, Pierre, 1968

[*La réfutation majeure*. English.]

The Major Refutation / Pierre Senges; translated from the French by Jacob Siefring

—1st Contra Mundum Press Edition
216 pp., 5 x 8 in.

ISBN 9781940625201

I. Senges, Pierre.
II. Title.
III. Siefring, Jacob.
IV. Translator.

2016959303

"Cet ouvrage, publié dans le cadre d'un programme d'aide à la publication, bénéficie de la participation de la Mission Culturelle et Universitaire Française aux Etats-Unis, service de l'Ambassade de France aux EU.

This work, published as part of a program of aid for publication, received support from the Mission Culturelle et Universitaire Française aux Etats-Unis, a department of the French Embassy in the United States."

TABLE OF CONTENTS

Editors' Foreword

The Major Refutation (Refutatio major, c. 1517 – 1525)

2 The Epistle Dedicatory

4 I: Overture

The solitude of the speaker — Initial reports at court of a great discovery — The speaker's initial acceptance of the claim — The credulity of the monarchs — The new world as an opportune object, convenient to all — The imposture goes unchallenged — The skepticism of the speaker — His nobility and his skepticism are one — The affinity of the speaker for the native who spurned his executors with a witty curse

12 II: Awaiting the Lame One

A new continent, much enlarged — Cartographers involved — The archives ransacked — "Everything that is fomented over there imitates our own fables" — "It could have been a question of more distant voyages and more radical metamorphoses" — "The invention of the new world will be built on that which forms the common bedrock of our conscience, the fear of the devil & the love of what gleams" — Thomas the Apostle, patron saint of skeptics — Thomas as the founder of an island colony

22   III: Men of Distances and Men of Letters

The new world a Spanish invention — As the fruit of Enrique IV's imagination — As the work of Isabella — Italy's involvement — France mostly aloof — Ottomans involved — The books of discovery are the works of the alchemists in disguise — Peter Martyr D'Anghiera — The Kabbalists — The new world a haven for the Jews — Apologia for Pope Joan

52   IV: The Litany of All That Gleams

The Polo brothers — Diverse accounts of travels abroad — The Waldseemüllers' workshops — Their strange methods — The Florentine workshops & their diverse attendance — Romances composed there — Painters and poets — The hermit painter Piero di Cosimo commissioned — Many evidences concocted — The natives exhibited in Spain — Christopher Columbus vilified — Amerigo Vespucci — Hernán Cortés — His philandering leads to a broken leg and a much delayed departure — Perennial disputes over the ownership of imaginary lands — "I have nothing of the colonist about me, Sire"

80   V: The Catalogue of Spoils

A great surplus of useless men — A method of population control — Planned shipwrecks — The Order of Alcántara involved — A local feud between Gómez de Solis and Alonso de Monroy — Honorific titles as incentives — Allegedly exotic diseases, namely the grand pox — "As if we had not already enough plagues" — The Jews persecuted — Church attendance in decline — The influence of Martin Luther — Luther an agent of the banks — The captivity and enslavement of the natives — The anti-slavery edict of 1477 and the ordinances of 1500 — The sadness and duplicity of the merchants — Courts of law and magistrates — "The law prevails" — The speaker's library — Spice wars — The new world as a strategy to defeat Venice — Gold and pepper mutually analogous — Counterfeits — The new world a promise and conjecture — Debts — The new world a promise of reimbursement — "My prince, be wary of gold-diggers"

112 VI: What Follows, et cetera

Land alchemy contrasted with seafaring alchemy — Inflations of currency — An ill economy — The speaker's purse — The new world as the abode of the dead

124 VII: Epilogue in Counterpoint

Lorenzo Valla praised — The tenacity of the dupes' beliefs — The dupes the most difficult to confute — Praise of Joanna the Mad for her skepticism — Certain dupes disillusioned — The speaker's apprehensions — Dupes and dupers conflated — The example of Diego Álvarez Chanca — Of acephalous men and their diverse characteristics — Prophecies

146 *Afterword*

On the peregrinations of Vâtsyâyana — Elements of bibliography — Myths, emblems, clues — Reconstitution — Major attribution: Antonio de Guevara — First minor attribution: Amerigo Vespucci — Second minor attribution: Joanna — Aphasia as dignity — Joanna the Mad, author of the Refutation — Other candidates considered — Rubrics from Lorenzo Valla — Conjecture as odyssey

182 *Coda*

Foreword

In the ship's log of Christopher Columbus (but rewritten almost entirely by Bartholomé de las Casas), at the entry dated Thursday, 11 October 1492, we read: *At two o'clock in the morning the land was discovered, at two leagues' distance. They took in sail and remained under the square-sail lying to till day, which was Friday, when they found themselves near a small island, one of the Lucayos, called in the Indian language Guanahani.*

In 1504, Amerigo Vespucci claims to have completed a fourth journey to the West Indies; in 1507, the name *America* appears for the first time on the Waldseemüller map. In 1512, Juan Ponce de Léon takes the Taíno Arawaks of the Bahama archipelago under his wing; in 1513, Núñez de Balboa discovers the Pacific.

Charles V is proclaimed king in 1516, at St. Gudula, in Brussels; three years later, he is unanimously elected emperor (but the Brandenburg elector takes care to record in a notarized statement that his vote was cast in fear). He travels widely, from Guadix to Ghent — he is supposed to have slept, by some accounts, in over 3,200 different beds, on land and at sea (moreover, it was his habit to bring his uncomfortable folding camp-bed along with him wherever he went: he was a king who slept in the rough).

It is commonly supposed that Antonio de Guevara, confessor to Charles V, composes his *Refutatio major* sometime between 1517 (the year Luther publishes his ninety-five theses) and 1525 (the year young Charles steps into the ring to fight a bull named Mahomet).

In these years of euphoria linked to the great discoveries, the text openly "challenges the opinions of eminent authors," to use the expression of Lorenzo Valla. A handful of literati in Seville and some correspondents in Ferrara perhaps have the privilege of reading some excerpts from it; here and there some pages of it turn up in vulgate translation.

In 1558, the historiographer Francisco López de Gómara alludes to a Grande Réfutation without mentioning its subject or revealing its author's name — he considers it the work of an idiot, yet woven of exactitudes.

In 1529, Antonio de Guevara, then bishop of Guadix, publishes *The Dial of Princes, including the Golden Boke of Marcus Aurelius*: a collection of advice, apologues, formulas, and jibes addressed to rulers, inviting them, as so many others did in the same era, to a more just governance of the world. Guevara attributes the *golden boke* to Marcus Aurelius himself: a literary artifice that fools no one. The English philologist Meric Casaubon saw in that feint a foul imposture; as for Pierre Bayle, he simply called Guevara a forger.

Antonio de Guevara died in 1545, at Mondoñedo, probably from complications of fever. He never bothered to sign his *Refutatio major*, nor was a copy of it found in his archives.

FOREWORD

The text which follows is the English translation of *La réfutation majeure*, itself a French translation of the Refutatio major made from the Latin copy in the collection of the library of Grenoble (C 4853).

The Major Refutation

THE EPISTLE DEDICATORY

To Charles I of Ghent, who is as magnificent as I am lowly and disparate, formerly by chance, now by necessity; to Charles of Ghent who is the most extraordinary and by far the most fortuitously placed ruler Europe has ever seen on its soil, from Extremadura to the basins of Flanders to the ships of the Hansa; to Charles who, like a child dropped into the lions' den and brought up alongside his fellow creatures, converts innocence to knowledge and hastens to redress his lack of preparedness through more work and authority; to Charles who has no peer in taking the power held out to him by his ancestors, as if he were accepting no more than a slice of pineapple, and who is peerless as well in relinquishing it, or feigning to do so, within his palaces, where he vows his humble powers to the God he imagines, summons, or dismisses at will; to Charles the Burgundian who knew how to strike fear into the hearts of the Spanish before he subjugated them, giving to eternity the example of a sovereign boldly coming face to face with each of his subjects, because he knew how to appear in their eyes as both a demon and an ordinary man (and to deceive them on both accounts, but with ample guile); to Charles who knew how to trim his family tree, to never subordinate the demands of State to filial love, nor waver in judgement before complaints or appeals, including those of kith and kin — to Charles I of Ghent, the author dedicates the present book.

And if it be an impertinence to offer such a work to such a prince, because he does not spare the Spanish court either, 'tis probably yet another to remain anonymous; but the Anonymous who happens to be aware of his obligations as well as of his rights asks his sovereign to be magnanimous yet once more, as pertinent and parsimonious as a taster of poisoned plates, and to never confuse cowardice with what is just simple prudence. By contradicting a vast imposture, this small work affronts both the living & the dead, noble lords & the multitude; I am not however afraid to offer it to he who, of all the men present upon this earth, is the greatest beneficiary of the frauds that were quietly carried out shortly before he acceded to the throne. Nor am I afraid to see this book fade into darkness, because such is its fate, as it is the fate of us all; neither am I afraid to see Charles curse these pages when he delivers his final will and testament, because the sympathy that men have towards things and sometimes creatures never ceases to wax with age, not until the final minute. For my survival, I rely on the tolerance of a king who has likewise seen through all manner of illusions.

ONE
Overture

Trumped by so many fables passing for promises, and by that counterfeit coin which they will throw on my tomb after my death in stead of soil, I now have only solitude and the presentation of facts to fall back upon, each so exact. Solitude, that would be this chamber, or the reflection of my face in a mirror, or rather my sole power; the presentation of facts is this present book, which I am abandoning, but which will I hope have an effect like the needle's prick.

I was however one of the first to accept the idea of a new land, westerly situated, even reduced, even poor, even were it no more than a heap of ordure eternally picked at by gulls; my acceptance was a kind of enthusiasm, proof that something of my youthful self still remained inside my old, owlish body. Hardly had the navigators set foot on Spanish soil & doffed their hats before their rulers than I subscribed forthwith to their initial reports. They spoke of islands and of mountains; I heard their testimony pronounced in a mixture of naiveté and solemnity (that is, in a quavering voice) as methinks I would have listened at the repeal of a verdict or, coming from the mouth of a monolithic judge, a commutation of a penalty of death to one of exile. Present in the halls of the palaces at Toledo, I heard what can only be called sighs of lax relief at the announcement of the great discoveries, though one might have sooner expected reactions of curiosity, of passion, of fear, stirrings of disbelief promptly interrupted by evidence or by envy (no matter that it would be the curiosity of the spice merchant, the passion of soldiers, and the fear of ambassadors obsessed with the Grand Turk or Venice). We were thus privy to that tense calm which holds sway when the most expert burglars do the deed, for as they openly own their hand must never tremble, every thief's success relying on a serenity and an assuredness as false as they are firm.

For the Catholic Kings, the announcement of a new land so far outside their jurisdiction inspired some cheerfulness tempered by pragmatism and, so near to ennui, a simple acceptance of the facts: but an acceptance in proportion to their generosity and to their power. Not to be astonished at the existence of a new continent is, for a sovereign, to demonstrate that their sovereignty lords it over the laws of geography, if need be also those of physics, as it often already lords it over common sense and the simplest rules drawn from the Mosaic commandments. In sum, the credulity of Isabella and Ferdinand, and of a few ministers perched like parrots on either side of the royal couple is a form of contempt on par with their greatness; but each courtier who wishes to appropriate that particular form of credulity to himself just as soon lapses into ridicule, for there is naught great about him, but for his plumèd cap and his jabbering tongue. For men of war, the announcement of a new land signifies more missions and a hope of promotion; for priests, a challenge to the texts of the Bible, but perchance proof of the existence of paradise on earth; for investors, the certainty of a hundredfold return on their investment; for tutors and governesses, topics for conversation; for astrologers, a peripeteia to be seen in the zodiac that very night; for certain plenipotentiaries, something to distract them from tedious European conflicts without end. A situation whereby every individual may choose, with the utmost prudence and precision, the particular form his or her credulity will take, from start to finish.

Thus did every one, in that fusion of intimacy and public gathering proper to the life of the court (the gregariousness of army ants and the solitude of the stillborn, condemned to hang in limbo) machinate in a trice with their particular inclinations and their particular faith, just as in divers circumstances every man reconciles himself to his scruples, his self-love, or strikes a bitter bargain with convictions held from childhood on, in a like attitude of recoil, perhaps even of terror disguised as phlegm. For mine own part, silent except in private converse, attentive as a trained dog, neither less timorous nor avid than my brethren, I have tried hard to discover in the depths of my soul, among sundry recollections, readings, daydreams hardly worthy of an adult, but also true and treacherous intuitions such as are revealed to mystics in visions, the exact measure of credulity which I might enjoy: a credulity which might bring me a lasting peace, with which I would be prepared to live out the rest of my days. This path was certainly the wrong one, for my credulity instantly gave out, and took leave of me, just as my soul will depart my body, through my mouth or nostrils, some years hence from now.

(I spoke of enthusiasm, but now that my credulity has deserted me I wonder if it were not mostly fed on algebra, if it were not connected to mathematics, for after long reflection I believe it comparable to the stupor one feels in the presence of an axiom as obvious as it is indemonstrable.)

My credulity voyages far afield without me, and without me commoners from the cities and towns are embarking on rickety, tumbledown ships in the hopes of going off to make a fortune in other climes. And while an incalculable number of naifs are sailing toward the new world, risking their lives, smaller groups of marquises and men at arms are deliberating over the lands to be conquered, without ever leaving the court. They laud it, they embellish it; they consider it not a simple pastime, nay, they persuade themselves, and in some cases there is nothing more abject than men so persuaded, whether they be knights or no, noble or ignoble. They affect a discriminating air, they pucker their lips a little, but their appetites are plain for all to see, just like their fascination of good little children in the presence of marvels. For mine own part, I consider myself like those Spanish Grandees who would refuse to remove their hats before the king: I do not discover myself in the presence of the new world, which is itself said to have been discovered, indeed so many times, that I have it ever before me, cap-in-hand, a humble courtier heedful of my intransigence, forever a vassal to my skepticism. The hat I keep on my head might be a symbol inherited from those brazen nobles whose impertinence Isabella later brought to heel, but who were at the time too proud to renounce their elegance, who would be loath to die uncoiffed. When I look with scorn on this new world, this bald-pated world, my incredulity becomes my nobility, not only my right pleasure, but also my royal virtue and the application of that virtue; doubt is to me a kingly principle as well as the chief trait of my aristocracy. Were I to found a dynasty, steadfastly guarding its headgear, I should want for the family trait transmitted to each new generation to be that incredulity which is forged in the workshop of Hephæstus, the lame.

Permit me this one avowal before proceeding any further: among the numberless natives dreamed up by the mythmakers over the years, there is but one whom I admire or whose invention I approve. I have forgotten his name, but what does the name of a bit player matter so long as his imaginary existence on paper suits our purposes, and his manner of death as well, so vivid and apt; after all, only the last words that he spake need concern us. Impossible not to salute that native chief who refused baptism at death's door, in the flames of the pyre, so as not to have to see (quoth he) his executioners in paradise — an utterance that puts Spain to shame but pays honour to the scribe capable of insinuating so much wicked pride in a single reply. I approve the words of that exotic prince and, if I could, if I were given the choice, I would paraphrase them daily — because I do dread to see in heaven all those who so tormented me, and who never missed a single mass. (The most heroic is not to risk Hell, but to refuse Paradise with the hauteur it takes to refuse a sinecure in the provinces.)

TWO
Awaiting the Lame One

First, it was a reef, then a handful of rocky outcrops, then an island, then an archipelago: after which, it became a peninsula adjoining another land; by dint of exaggeration, the liars back from their voyages, the mapmakers and speculators reckoning profits on untold hectares of land, the preachers and missionaries involved too, together they transformed that peninsula into a country, that country into a continent. Ere long this continent will be a terrestrial globe, one quite like our own, on which we might go a-clambering: it would be the Moon, if we needed to swallow more such balderdash, our appetite for lies being so insatiable.

If this new world actually existed, if its measure could be had in hectares and in tons, or more maliciously in carats to reflect the value of its diamond mines, or in nautical miles because it is seemingly capable of devouring an entire hemisphere as a crab would, going from north to south and from east to west — if this were the case, then adventurers would have set foot there long ago, smugglers failing to find a better use for their discovery would have taken it as their refuge, & instead of traffickers by nature mute about their rallying points, we would have heard the cries of one thousand boasters, one thousand returning voyagers (the worst sort of boatmen become roosters or peacocks again, the worst sort of pilgrims with all their old age after the voyage to crow over their adventure, till their saliva runs out or their tongues drop off). Who wouldn't have discovered it, that land glimpsed from a mast's height by the unfortunate Rodrigo de Triana (whom I knew in Bougie when he was a shoemaker, and then as a wax vendor, and a straw man to numerous trials): María la Brava would have been able to row there to avenge her sons by bringing back a hundred of those nutmeg-coloured natives' heads on stakes, María la Brava would have been able to land there if the madness of her vengeance had propelled her there, panting for breath, or if someone, to throw her off the scent, had told her that her children's killers were hiding out there, where the sun goes down. Perchance Enrique IV would have made it to the same territory if Spain's Grandees, grown weary of his listless and soapy airs, had set him in a barque and the currents borne him away to those territories. Afonso V would have been able to reach it, if the future Queen Isabella had demanded that he circle the globe in order to find the gardens of Paradise as the sole location conducive to their honeymoon. Holland's drapers would have been able to reach that land if they had divined a loyal and reliable clientèle there, or some silkier, more velvety competition; lastly, the young Marco Polo, followed by his brothers, could have reached it if the Great Khan, wherever he stood, had raised a finger, with the nonchalant air of a pasha whose authority seems taxed by the least gesture, to point the way to a country large as a whale. You yourself, my excellent prince, you could go there today with nary a concern for the vast expanses to be traversed: despite all of my objections, the existence of this country would ultimately depend on your powers and on your imagination.

To paint the portrait of this new territory, the mapmakers in their workshops are drawing free-hand sketches of coastlines that are not a whit newfangled, but for their way of appraising our world scornfully, as if from a foreign shore. Bringing islands into existence on paper is a heady game: I have taken it up myself in order to appreciate such intoxication as trumpery procures, that of an adventure on the high seas, at hardly any cost, drawn out in the meticulous outline of gulfs, hills, natural harbours, headlands, capes, deltas, swamps, bone-heaps and rocks peopled with grey fowls; it sufficed to set some corsairs gamboling there. But the mapmakers go further: they invent the natives of these territories too, drawing their faces in the manner of the Guanches of the Canaries, or Ukrainians driven by force to Genoa; without inventing much they invent loincloths copied from Madeira, shoes copied from Ceylon, and sticks of incense copied from Bactria but placed in the mouth. As for the amorous rites of the natives, the clerks in Isabella's workshops only had to leaf through the ledgers of the Old and New Inquisitions, but also the works of Tertullian, where he denounces the excesses of the Gnostics & their collective mating practices, involving devorations, anthropophagy, child sacrifices, sodomies complicated by the age of the subjects and their numerousness. They plunge into these annals as if into the reservoir of all possible combinations, the imagination being for them but a principle of permutations, and nothing else. The Cathars, before they retracted, addressed their torturers with periphrases we find almost unchanged in the accounts of many impostors returned from the New Indies. We can see that the promoters of these lands under the horizon did not have to look very far for their lying words, which they simply cut from books, sometimes with their images, combining them freely with those old lullabies that our grandmothers recite now and then, no longer believing in them, but transmitting them all the same since one must talk of something if only to fill the day's idle hours.

By reading these works, by plundering the archives, in other words by resurrecting these long dormant voices, each can see for himself that this world arbitrarily pulled out of the sea is neither a new idea, nor an ingenious invention of our admirals, but rehashed legends, dressed up in drama and luxury to appeal to modern appetites, embellished sometimes with the help of parades of passive, nude savages, insinuated by the conquerors — the sole novelty these crude, chronically celibate men are capable of inventing to excite their fantasies, nay, the consummation of these fantasies in a tightly clenched fist, since love, discovery, and imagination are for them matters of force. No one can convince us that the Atlantic islands are an original idea, or that sailors from Lisbon or Genoa are telling for the first time of western archipelagoes adrift on the tenebrous sea. There are in our libraries so many allusions to Atlantis, to the voyages of St. Brendan, to the Seven Cities, to Ante Illa and to the island of Brazil; so many now tattered books tell of the drifting of the Apostles of God toward the unbelievers and scorpions of the east and of the west, so many tattered books describe the walls of legendary cities and islands in the shape of tortoises: you would swear that the adventure of the new world were naught else than a hardly embellished copy of our old legends, a copy graven on the sea, instead of on paper: farce for farce, we could have been just as glad with a book.

Everything that is fomented over there imitates our own fables; we will then have to resign ourselves to seeing the imaginary beings migrating irresistibly toward the west, which the conquerors claim to occupy and administer, as best they can. Not content to have situated the Indies where the sun sets, they expatriate the islands of Ulysses there too and maybe the rocks of Charybdis; soon we will hear a boast more boastful than the rest, and more in line with the arts of promotion, informing us that the Britannic Isles have dropped anchor 370 leagues to the west of Cape Verde, that they neighbour Flanders, and that a sailor who sails from Lisbon in a crow's nest and keeps a straight course will eventually reach the port of Anvers and its remarkable clouds. We will be told that Paris is a famous city in these archipelagoes, of which the city in France is but the reflection, produced by a trick of mirrors, or a copy, shimmering in the water's surface.

The elucubrations of these copyists seek to marvel the reader with flashes of the gold of Chersonesos, but on the whole they only look like paltry glosses, as dry as a commentary on the Song of Songs by an abbot castrated at birth. What I find most astonishing is not so much the credulity of my contemporaries as the austerity of their credulity, the confined aspect that their imaginations take on when the inventors & cartographers employ dreams for such few and limited possibilities: a handful of islands, some disreputable indigenes and a few vegetables. Instead, it could have been a question of more distant voyages and more radical metamorphoses: the fomenters of these new lands could have followed line by line the tales of Christine de Pizan, who composed her long voyage without ever leaving her room. And rather than repeating that the earth is round, and sticking to this simple idea, why not assert with Cosmas Indicopleustes that our world has the form of a Tabernacle, held aloft by angels at each of its corners? We could have gone riding around on seahorses or centaurs, we could have mingled ourselves with trees and known the life of the forest; the discoverers of the new world could have brought back love stories theretofore unthinkable, for coupling man with that which he least resembles. Instead, apart from our old tales revisited long ago by Pliny and our own Isidore of Seville, they speak of naught but commerce, of gold mines, of fruits harvested and sold, of investment and return on investment; and when it's not the language of commerce, it's the language of the Basoche or of clerks in the charge of State, thus a matter of confidential reports, of administrations, of fiefs, of full powers and half-powers, of delegations, of missions, of governance and of diplomacy; and when not the language of the State it's the language of the Church, which sets its missionaries hopping, and tries with pathetic violence to interest a vast population of dupes in questions of the soul

& of paradise (especially the question of whether the islands imprudently invented by the conspirators be compatible with Scripture; but there are so many obscure passages in the Bible that it is within the reach of any clever person to find an allusion to lands impossible to fix on a map, if not in Elias, then in Proverbs, and if not in Proverbs, then in Job — & if not Job, Revelation).

The new world, an enchantment? however when John Day, a good sailor no doubt, but a geographer of little import, announces that somewhere to the west islands have been found where "grass grows," he is either smirking with deceit, or mocking our rulers, to whom he extends an offer of six square yards of lawn in the guise of a vast kingdom. These men go off into the horizon, where they lose their heads, exert themselves furiously, ravish Indian women, move mountains and entire populations, drown a thousand sailors in their wake, and then come back to us, swearing in magnificent syllables that grass grows on these lands and that in their environs, by the grace of God, rain falls down from on high. Sire, you who know how to open your heart to all the rumours of the world, and if not your heart, your mouth, whereby the Creator insufflates our soul, you will know how to turn a deaf ear to such confabulators.

For so it often goes: certain instigators of paradise, once they sober up and no longer have a Dominican by their side to top off their glass, forget about the marvellous gardens, conjured from the tip of a plume, forget about the aviaries and the nude ballets, instead recount more sordid bacchanals, dull &

lugubrious festivities, and their menageries empty out, their bestiaries are deserted, the fantastic plants become ordinary clover and nettle again, and they find themselves back on the dusty sands of our La Mancha, where we begin, where we will all end: three times nothing. Michele di Cunéo paints a delicious portrait of this paradise for us, with its angels and fertile gardens, though with the modesty and restraint of a man who finds himself freshly sober: the natives over there grow vegetables with roots like those of our turnips (he claims), they grate them for pies. So many enchanting and dumbfounding fantasies to unsettle the least credulous among them, shuffle them onto a caravel, and lead them on to damnation; and, if there were not on this side of the globe the hosts of our churches to keep our old Christians pacified, maybe even I myself, finally conquered and glad to be so, I would have made the leap and gone off to those newfound islands to besot myself with turnips, sell my soul for them, no less.

Simple minds need to be given to dream though: invention must then rely on exaggeration, the swindle on the value of the promised reward, the spice merchant's income on the size of the profit which he promises his victims (and which he calculates with a worried air — as if he were constructing the raft on which both he and his mark would save their skins); the invention of the new world will be built on that which forms the common bedrock of our conscience, the fear of the devil and the love of what gleams. To enlighten the beggars of Spain and Holland, the divulgers had the good sense to have the natives march about at fairs, their bellies exposed &

covered in paint, uttering not a word — and when the beggars slapped their thighs and gaped like fish, their aim was more or less accomplished. Sometimes even surpassed: divulgation becomes charlatanry, whose sole function is to gauge the credulity of the client, a good taxpayer then, on into penury. Likewise could I inform my compatriots, whether they be circumspect or dupes, that one of the proofs of the non-existence of a new continent is the presence on its soil (conjectured by John of Holywood) of blue creatures with square heads.

If the lies contradict themselves, and the dupes who stay behind start to find them hard to swallow (as if one were asking us to believe the world were a turtle stacked atop another turtle and thus to infinity), then the fabulists recuse themselves, they stick to the most likely scenario — grass and pebbles, we saw it — or leave things vague. The extraordinary islands, which no one believes in any longer, they prefer to modestly shroud in permanent mists, thus the Island of the Siete Ciudades, whose fog (they tell us presently) remains impenetrable. But all of this idle talk comes to an end: when the colonists are returned to Spain, disappointed to have reaped only crosswinds, misery, and drizzles, when they see Christopher Columbus, they address him as *Admiral of Mosquitoes*, another way of saying that he in truth ruled over none but the stagnant marsh air; a way, also, of indicating that the voyages are naught but torments, that instead of gold sequins, the travellers bring back insect bites, fevers that do not subside. I have heard so many lamentations from so many cheated sailors, I could give you a staggering summary of them: if you doubt my word, you can go into the marketplaces of Seville and hear grape-vendors, who were yesterday rich hidalgos ready for all manner of adventure, now calling the continents relegated to the other side of the horizon, "the land of vanity and deceit." And I know that to delay the truth some additional weeks, the impostor Columbus, himself a puppet of others, incited all of his men, fake sailors but genuine debauched peasants, to lie, shewing them continents or peninsulas where there were only reefs: threatened with a fine of ten thousand maravedís, or the blows of the rod, or having their tongues cut out, they were made to recite, once they were back to port, the lessons they learned on the bridge, in the middle of the sea.

Even my worst enemy, in the person of Peter Martyr d'Anghiera, whose overly prolific writings confirm the imposture as a *lettre de cachet* confirms a sentence, even this enemy of mine speaks in his *Decades* of a hypothetical continent (*creido continente*). But I know of no more severe judgement regarding the imaginary lands than those three lines lost at sea on the mappa mundi of the honourable Johannes Ruysch, according to whom the isle of Antilia was discovered by the Portuguese long ago: "now when we look for it, we cannot find it." What is most remarkable is not this mosaic of signs and petty witnesses which the mercenaries bring back from Cape Verde to cozen their sedentary counterparts, but the braggart ostentation with which they brandish the counter-proofs, as if the better to subjugate, then triumph, then renege; our fake nobles and gilded youth strut themselves with less arrogance than that.

That horizon, behind which the promoters have made islands rise up, placed Indians who are not Indians, dogs that are not dogs, tribes of Israel that are not tribes of Israel, and birds not quite the same as our birds — I would gaze out at it from the beach, sitting long hours, my back erect, beside neighbours more tense and silent than myself if they were imagining to themselves this new world's portrait, or more silent still if listening inwardly to the voices of their consciences. Chance companions: many of us were trying hard to maintain a humble stillness, and perhaps we would have attained it if the cold, the day's end, weariness (and other demands) had not required us to quit our watch; I believe that our rock-hard incredulity consoled us for there being behind that horizon, in front of us, nothing but a vast expanse in which we might lose ourselves, one by one.

Others who share my incredulity and, why not put it thus, my rank, might someday choose St. Thomas the Skeptic as their tutelary figure; following his example, they will probe for a wound in order to dispel all manner of doubt, but also to distinguish blood from a simple red dye, and so doing, they will add pain to pain, for a fingernail charged with keeping the truth of a stigmata in check cannot help but tremble. Likewise, I too would choose Thomas, and be his itinerant companion, following in the footsteps of the apostle and the wandering Jew alike, because the penance of all doubters is to walk ever onwards. What is most pathetic is that such interminable wandering risks leading me, if I am to believe these commentators, more or less directly to the edges of the new world: because it is precisely there that one chronicler affirms having discovered a tribe of people dwelling in eternal peace & praying to Thomas as their original founder. The Doubter would have gone ashore at the end of his long voyage in those realms, after having frequented regions where unreliable witnesses saw him, with the Parthians, in Persia, or off the Malabar Coast; towards the end of his life he would have set down his valise on that improbable continent, and founded a new clan by marrying a girl of the country, perhaps a child of the lost tribes of Israel, perhaps a descendant of Lilith. Henceforth it would be said: St. Thomas peopled this world by bringing his version of the Gospel here, as well as his seed: but wouldn't it be somewhat fatal to turn the Doubter into the founding father of those overseas lands? and would it not be the height of buffoonery to invite travellers, immediately upon arrival, to inspect from such proximity the irrefutable proof of his presence in those parts?

THREE
*Men of Distances
and
Men of Letters*

You are the most well placed, my prince (that is to say, on the throne), to know that this great wile concerns Spain in the utmost, because it is under its banner that the ships churn the waters to foam. Spain? improvised heroisms, not the less admirable therefor; greedy knaves playing all out, ready to drown themselves if a fire is lacking and ready since boyhood to slash the throats of infidels whenever they are in season, all the way to Granada; knights with beards such as mercenaries for the conquest will later sport, made to rehearse the roles they will play in the new world; six-foot-tall soldiers, accompanied by grammarians, functionaries, and annalists (the country's unity supposing an armada of idle, learnèd men); old Catholics, jealous of their jealous God, gleaning pieces of the true cross; jurists theorizing on the purity of blood; Jews disguised, dead, or humiliated by the waters of baptism, delivered into the sea. Also it is the country of Maria la Brava, bringing back from her long voyage the impaled heads of the two young men who assassinated her sons; the country of Enrique IV, soft, introverted, abulic, perhaps prognathous because for painters and for caricaturists, an aberration of the mind is matched by one of the body. It's the country of military and religious orders, of thrice-sworn knights and priests ready to help with a finely calibrated scale to divvy up the spoils of war (the *quito del rey* set wisely off to the side); the country of Alcántara, parading its wealth and its armed forces through the streets like lunatics publicly declaiming their *idées fixes*, and watching as Alonso de Monroy and Gómez de Solís face off for its leadership; the country where men poison each other, where the dread powder of succession enervates inheriting princes, future sons-in-law, fiancés who imprudently reserve beds in inns located in the middle of the desert. It's the country of financial calculations where, in the manner of a zero represented by a point (after the ancient method of the Arabs), men sometimes cross the border and are immediately reduced to nothing if the algebraic operation requires it; the country where a fubsy half-sailor known as Columbus, not quite pious, imperfectly cynical, serves the Catholic Kings and their people a blatant lie. Grotesquely, it is the country where Cortés, on the eve of his first departure, is caught with his pants down in the bed of a married woman, escapes out the window, breaks his leg, renounces his travel plans, then spends two years vacationing on the roads of Italy with rapier in hand or in the depths of a library to study botany, according to divergent reports. At the heart of this kingdom, my prince, you are as solid and immovable as the Caudine Forks in the chaotic crush of a carnival crowd.

To most observers, the invention of the new world would appear to be the work of Spain, that Spain which John II, Ferdinand, and Joanna delivered into your hands. Numerous soldiers and bishops fled from Italy and its wars; they fled the magnanimity of Louis XII and the Borgias in the vicinity of Capua, a magnanimity soon converted into the murder of thousands of men, the rape of twice as many women and petty haggling in Rome's marketplaces over the price of orphans, brats no doubt, but none the less profitable for being so. Some half-soldiers, hucksters, and intellectuals were given refuge at the court of the Catholic Kings, your ancestors, and, because they found nothing past that land (once Galicia is reached, all that remains is to go drown in the Atlantic), these voluntary exiles stayed right where the wind had set them down, ready from then on for all manner of adventure, as soon as we gave them the opportunity to wriggle forth. The invention is a Spanish gambit, as surely as that mélange of riff-raff and poets, one-armed crooks and savants as sly as serpents successfully foments a new world, first discretely in their inner circles for their own consolation and diversion, then openly, by word of mouth, taking great care to regulate the balance of the informed to the ignorant, for the secret is diluted among the multitude and it fades away in confidentiality. The invention depends on the impatience of knights, on the fervor of the military and religious orders, the ardour of peasants and, in very large part, on ruined hidalgos, ready to do anything to regain their honour, even go off and steal an egg from the Roc bird's nest, or the gold leaves which garland it. It depends on the Fuggers' and the Walsers' capital, granted first as an irrecoverable loan, later recouped with interest; it depends on the imagination of bankers, eager to admit the existence of a new continent if they can be assured that their debts will be repaid; it will depend later on the manœuvres of your Grand Chancellor Mercurino Gattinara, at your bedside, Sire, a flatterer according to whom you are the universal monarch, an absolute king to whom God himself will come to pay homage, by deposing several rolls of satin at your feet.

These New Indies (a desolate landscape, as described by the coarsest peasants), I have long supposed to be the fruit of the demented imagination of King Enrique IV, dubbed the Impotent: a listless imagination, dulled but exaggerated by sloth and idle time, strengthened even by that languor, and grown fertile in a most disagreeable way. It draws force not from what is powerful and immediate, but from what is persistent and lasting, as seemingly eternal as the days, the dust, and the shifting of the sands. I have long thought that the new lands are a phantasmagoria of that lamentable prince, belonging to the same order as those half-woman half-fish chimaeras, spectres, or succubi which he could not resist conjuring as he sat atop his throne, presiding over the world with a puny sceptre in hand, from time to time dropped, when he was summoning to his side, for want of friends to invite, the most misbegotten phantoms that ever tempted Anthony (for his part, he was as unyielding as rock).

An imagination, which is and is not that of a hermit after forty days' fasting, abstinence and immobility (or an exaggerated pantomime thereof; for, in the absence of demons and she-devils, the abulic prince was obliged to act out for himself alone a shew in their image, with marionettes, which Cisneros later burned with Torquemada as his witness). Enrique the Impotent, who set the ugliness of his face upon a throne as hollow as his head, and who spent his evenings getting his full hour's worth, doubtlessly decided one fine day to bring into existence, towards the sunset, at the far end of the world, a beach of sand, a void beach, as the outward image of his own mind.

A *mundus novus?* the imaginary of an abulic no doubt, nothing appearing truer or in a certain way more real than a new continent, begotten in the vapours of a lazy afternoon, intoxicating, doleful, in the solitude of a king with neither court nor sovereignty, a groom without nuptials who buckles as soon as he draws near to his bride, as others do at the Ocean's edge or at the world's furthest extremity. From a man so thoroughly stricken by non-desire as this, skilled enough to make it into a cast of mind, a metaphysick, a poetry, because he transforms his disposition into a profession of faith — from a man stricken by a stupor, which is not that of satanists, nor that of heretics, nor that of the possessed, but the stupor of an idiot king who has accomplished every thing whilst doing absolutely nothing, or read his fortune in a book day in day out, and who would want to guard against reliving a life already set down in such minute detail —, from such a man, surely, I do expect the invention of a new world, both present *&* absent, dependable *&* deceptive, new *&* older than Abraham, recorded in Scripture and absent from its pages, a country in the form of destiny and of accident, unearthed with much ado and discovered by chance, a paradise but a desert, where naked but not obscene men go about with reserve but without virtue; a world occupied by gods who will finally have to be slaughtered because they proved, by their weakness, their belonging to humanity.

One might suppose however the *mundus novus* and its dusting of isles to be a machination of Isabella alone, who not only reinstated the Office of the Inquisition and reanimated the cadaver of Bernardo Gui by strapping wooden shafts to its arms, but also knew how to succeed where Frederick II of Hohenstaufen had failed before, to wit, by laying siege to an old city & building around it a new city, in order to surround and enstrangle it, whilst erecting towers from blueprints as aligned with the classical logic of war as with the logic of urban design. I am of course talking about the siege of Santa Fe which, at the end of the Spanish soil, effectively reduced Islam to a handful of deserters, racing to the strait to thrash about in the waters before drowning; Isabella oversaw the destruction of the old city and the construction of the new one with the arrogance of a chevalier-king having his way with the world. It was surely there that she first conceived of a plan for the conquest to come, or rather for a world to be fabricated from start to finish. Henceforward, conquerors will no longer be just calamities associated with the fall of cities, but also calamities by which other cities will be raised up; and not just cities, but countries and continents too; islands will be seen floating up out of the water, like prodigious shards of wreckage.

Isabella, I hardly knew her when death was still far from her; I saw her profile only once: a lovely little figure in a locket, the portrait of a woman whom one wouldn't suspect would bite Europe's heel, put Venice in shackles, and join Castile to Aragon behind the bonnet of the King of Portugal. She is considered, and I approve this judgement, intrepid but sedentary, violent without raising her voice, pious but not scraping her knees on the stones of any cloisters, and trusting to others to wear the veil. She is one of those combustible spirits, at once terrorized and terrible: lucid but on the verge of letting go, capable, like those double-sided portraits (a young girl on one side, a shrew on the other), of transforming themselves in an instant, of risking all for all, risking madness without a single change ever appearing in her speech or her outward disposition, swinging as a pendulum from ambition to extravagance or from authority to autarky, from originality to idiocy. Hardly insane, Isabella knew to err on this side of reason, & thus she delegated to her subordinates, her vassals, her inheritors, the obligation to be mad on her behalf, to pray the rosary or agonize over the passage of time, whilst watching the hour hand in its journey round the still nave.

This panorama, from Toledo to Córdoba, will I hope please you, you who have always known how to be Spanish among the Bourguignons, and Bourguignon at the court of Castile. But, at bottom, maybe the invention is not exclusively Spanish, and conspiracies of Roman or Florentine origin are afoot beyond this country's borders, of which Spain is the sole dupe, or the tool, and the Catholic Kings simple foils, costermongers charged with delivering the goods. Though my mind was carried by suspicion, I nevertheless attentively lent my ear to the messengers from here and abroad who said that tattered Italy, golden in places, bloody and inflamed in others, has at its disposition, all across Europe, seated in its taverns, a network of poets accompanied by merchants who divulge all that one can know of the new world in the form of sailor's legends, drinker's tales, official letters, account books shewing incredible profits, and maps of the world. For years, centered around Florence (it is said), agencies staffed by charlatans, drunkards, or alchemists besotted with ether, which they suck in during their chants, are writing and rewriting the memories of navigators returning from the west: accounts from Vespucci, for example, which they exaggerated in every regard. All the glass jewelry they brought back, the gold, the feathers, the silver, the miracles, the girls in loincloths and the slaves playing reed-pipes, all of that not sufficing, the persuasion must be effected through public readings, & above all by confidences: the surest way to spread a secret around while flattering the pride of one's confidants (they love to count themselves part of a tiny circle whose members they count on their fingers). In Florence, Vespucci polished the book of his travels with such care that he soon gained a reputation as one of the discoverers of the so-called useless islands, legend having initially attributed that prestigious title to a blowsy halfwit named Columbus (who soon got in the way, and was just as soon put in his place). That's how it goes: the official versions of the discovery square off on land just like the fleets at sea, such that it is now common to consider this Vespucci, Florentine *flōrentissime*, sword-bearer for the Medicis, like the rival of Columbus the Genoan, a rather maladroit, overly devout commoner down to his ship's log. In the contest between Amerigo and Christopher, the amused onlookers see Florence's war with Genoa playing itself out anew, an eternal misfortune: they amuse themselves by counting the dead.

We have also suspected enemies from Venice and even the Papal States, who have always been taken by great febrility. Whereas France, on the contrary, has been placid from the start: perhaps because that country is inhabited by skeptics and arguers, dry trees insusceptible to the charms of the imagination, while a sanguine people beyond the Pyrenees have allowed themselves to be seduced by tales of nutmeg and girls stepping out of the bath. Perhaps because that cold country is so frugal, except when it is lusting after Empire and bribing the Grandees, because it shews itself parsimonious in everything and sometimes in thought, and would only admit the existence of African elephants if they deigned to come by foot from Carthage, to present themselves at the king's court and kneel down betwixt two chamberlains. Perhaps because that country has long been sufficient unto itself and is satisfied with a harbour for doing its groceries, and a port or dry dock for admiring its fleet, but abstains from envisioning marvellous spice markets at the far end of the world. Or maybe because that country of clerics and soldiers — roughneck soldiers with used virtue for hire — is presently preoccupied with Italy, where they have their own Eldorado, their deserts, their legendary towns and cities to pillage, mother superiors to gut to enliven their history books. Or rather because that country as supercilious as a cardinal's frock, muddy and encrusted as its hem, finds contentment in the Mediterranean, spurns the Atlantic & its unfindable islands, prefers a closed basin where it can keep on sending its fleet round in circles as it has for a long time, negotiating the price of oil from Sfax and pistachios from Riad, for those are the gold nuggets it prefers, and otherwise trafficking with the Mamelukes.

Finally, I would not deny those who, touched by the manœuvres of Mehmed II, point out how malicious the Turks can be: their success on the battlefields, on the Danube, on the Dniester, on the shores of the Black Sea, are not at all incompatible with diplomatic ruses. According to them, the new world is an invention of Bayezid, son of Mehmed, a sort of vast Ottoman mirage orchestrated by certain impostors infiltrating the embassies, acting with the help of certain traitors, whose goal is to throw the Christian navies for a loop. All the armadas engaged in the Ocean among its sirens effectively fail Venice when it is attacked by the Turkish fleet, just as Durazzo and the Peloponnese were before. 'Tis said that those whom the Spanish chased off the coast of Cape Verde were Bayezid's janissaries, and that it was the sultan's concubines who were exhibited to the Catholic Kings, disguised as island girls — but certain strategists went mad from imagining that an Ottoman stood behind every charming enchantment.

Notwithstanding the conspiracies that have ensued, that are still unfolding, notwithstanding such fulsome plottings, I have been led to wonder if the cause of the invention were not a misunderstanding. I can confidently impute the origin of that which is presently tormenting us to a small book, printed in Venice as they just about all seem to be these days, the city sinking down a little more with each stamp of the press. A book which is the first to speak of a new land, of a virgin continent, of useless islands, of discoveries, of Ante Illa, of Eldorado of course, and of numerous other creatures, the names of which have since been recited to no end (an act to which I resign myself willingly because it is not bad to intone extraordinary words from time to time, for our convalescence). This book, the size of the tiniest sextodecimo missals (to tell the truth quite mediocre in conception), even if it seems to speak of voyages and distant journeys, and refers unambiguously to the west, and the sunset where gold and fire are combined under the effects of heat, even if it speaks of a river carrying sparks of light, if it speaks of a journey, an initiation, of tempests and boilings, if it imagines or promises unknown territories, never before visited, if it foretells the transformations effected to white creatures through their contact with black creatures and red creatures, if it also suggests the world's hidden surfaces and latent riches infinitely superior to the spice stocks of Portugal (a stick of cinnamon is nothing in comparison to quicksilver), this mediocre book is contrary to appearances not the journal of a sailor, it is a treatise on alchemy, such as are produced in great numbers these days in line with works by Pierre Vicot and Basile Valentine, a book that someone hoped would secure them a fortune, at least editorially: instead of distilling drinkable gold, it set rivers of ink aflow.

Therein we read of the work, of stone, of volatile gold, except that whatever anonymous party had the book printed, on certain pages quite crookedly, thought it wise to spin a maritime metaphor, with good reason we might add, seeing as the worst alchemists and spice merchants everywhere think in terms of commodities and profits, cutting wholes into parts in order to multiply value tenfold, before repeating the operation. More, the alchemist like the merchant prefers a mathematic whereby each numeral is symbolized by a gold token, which should be news to no one; the two love mystery, the one on the sea, the other in his lair; they are harried spectators, they see exoticism at their door, they imagine they are approaching the Orient of monsters they've always known existed, or think that the devils described by St. Augustine will materialize from the smoke of their ovens. They also both have an immoderate love of foreign languages, Phoenician dialects or the writing of the Egyptians; they share the sentiment that cryptography aids them in their quests and shields them from the profane, while also invigorating science, because Greek roots pepper their discourse, in the way the mandrake root spices up the dialogue of old couples.

These books, alchemical tomes, rely on too many mixed metaphors, like certain unimpeachable saints who consort with too many demons or archangels. They rub elbows with so many formulas, contiguous with truth, by which they aim to truss up their audience but in which they themselves end up entangled: crows, fires, stars, wheels, red and black eagles, rain showers, snakes, flasks and antlers are and are not their instruments, are and are not manifest, exist or do not exist upon their worktables. Everyone knows, anyways, that the alchemist's goal is to deceive his reader, that such a leading astray is regularly an end in itself, & that any attempt to curb that trickery would be vanity itself, with the reason being that the void of our existence waits for us on the other side of every enigma, once its solution will have been found. The alchemist hides, but rarely, a single verity in a forest of signs, parceling it out, introducing the end before the beginning, truncating formulas that refer to an untraceable ancillary volume, the sole copy in a library in Parma, destroyed by fire; by such a poetics of redundancy, he drives his less diligent disciples to exhaustion, and is visibly proud to play like that and in other vile ways, whether on marble or in the gruel; and when he is sure that the amphigory will have gotten the better of everyone's patience and nearly everyone will have forgotten, only then does he release a pin's worth of his science.

Because they have exhausted their images, certain authors, weary of having to evoke the same hackneyed allegories for the hundredth time (the Stone, the Fountain, the Moon, the Taurus, and the Scale), have sooner preferred to describe their art or its object as though it were a country: possessing two shores like the two sides of truth, forests analogous to impenetrable calculation, mountains like facts to be bypassed, volcanoes to evoke sleeping fire or muted vivacity. They spoke of faraway isles to intimate to their initiates that the work of alchemy is far more frequently a shipwreck than a voyage, for failure is, along with that shadow and that cold like no other that hold sway around a white-hot stove, the savant's sole companion, his most loyal friend. They speak of the west to suggest poetically that the sun of truth reaches it by a process of combustion, that it bonds with it before dissolving, illuminates the misguided before seething to a boil; they speak of reefs beyond the horizon as many others before them have spoken of elusive birds or headless serpents; and with the crashing of waves against the shore, they evoke our intuition, which incessantly laps up against simple and straightforward facts, before receding ever anew; they speak of desolate lands close to paradise in order to remind us that aridity is the neighbour of fecundity; they speak of marvellous but hostile fauna on these shores to recall the incompatibility of mercury and copper sulfate; they speak of nuggets brought back from inaccessible lands to suggest that pure gold is the sole aim of the reddening phase, and that all of their figures of rhetoric, in fact, refer but to it.

Hermeticism, as the invention of the new world, is based on the hypothesis that a truth is degraded in the very instant it is revealed, it having no other purpose than to occult some all the more rare, thus all the more valuable, verity; for ages now initiates, passing from revelation to revelation, have striven to thwart the layman. So do hermetic, ultimately vain pursuits possess the charm of westerly voyages, in the direction of a land situated behind the horizon, that is to say just under it: they always require us to keep going beyond if we want to see.

(It remains to be seen how the doctrine of correspondences errs when it so generously involves the author and his followers in a ballet of signs, of facts, of words, and of epithets, in such great quantity that the multiplication of links between individual parts yields a tautology, experienced as a revelation.)

The little sextodecimo book was roughly in the same vein: it treated of alchemical affairs in terms of navigation, cordage, & geography. Certain naive persons, such as are to be found everywhere, have taken these utterances for their watchwords: they pride themselves on setting the literal higher than the metaphorical sense; they have departed like solitary men going off to drown themselves in the setting sun.

The gods or chance have bestowed on you, Sire, the wisdom of Solomon, the authority of Jacob, and above all the discretion of Philoctetes; you will be able to hear, I believe, the confidences of one of your servants, a simple witness, without betraying him.

I have done my best to lead a quiet life; I have tried to direct my attention only to modest objects, those which appear fleetingly before vanishing, like the flicker of gold on the horizon at a certain hour of day, and have tried to imagine myself rich with all that escapes me, I have tried to savour my losses and failures; I do not believe that I harbour a grudge, nor that I let my melancholy spur me to crusade against mitered asses and laureled macaques. No one will see me waving my arms: if my deception is immense, if my griefs, like those of my peers, appear to know no limit and to voyage around the world all of their own accord, my response to the fables will be just these marginal notes, especially the proper reading that you hope to make of them. I would never challenge an individual like Peter Martyr d'Anghiera to a duel, and I will not try to lure him into an ambush; it is almost with reticence that I intend to shew right here and now that he is an exemplary traitor, or accomplice, the obedient apostle of the new world, the apocryphal Gospels of which he composes with pathetic zeal.

Peter Martyr d'Anghiera: the clerk in the service of the cause, religious by chance, routine, or habit, the most clever quill carrier of kings, ambassadors, landowners, generals, on certain occasions a penman for merchants and creditors, in brief for all those who have fomented, clumsily at first, the *mundus novus*, all those who have an interest in there being a land alternately mixing bread-fruit trees, fountains of gold, subjugated natives and birds like notions of monsters thrown down on paper in colourful inks. Peter Martyr is the petty poet of the imposture, the fanatical clerk of the court, industrious, at his worktable when everyone else quits and goes home to bed, a man convinced that the lies he dreams up in daylight will go on living at night, of their own accord, like those demons which overworked persons conceive between wakefulness and sleep. (And if, many nights, I too keep vigil into the small hours, with or without valour, agitated by boyish passion or by the nervosity of the old curmudgeon I consider it my duty to be, if I pass white nights, if I outlive my last candle, if I await the return of the sun as a sign that life continues and not as a proof of the earth's rotundity, it is so that I can claim to be the one and only partner of this sly, ingenuous Peter Martyr, who never seems to sleep, he neither, it is to play my part on this earth symmetrically, as if a monstrous hand had interposed a mirror betwixt myself and him. It would be extraordinary to lead in a like manner the life of an antipope.)

It was initially pity that led me to take an interest in the situation of Peter Martyr, who appeared to mine eyes as an enslaved scribe, ultimately deprived of his critical faculties as Sima Qian, the official historian of the Han dynasty, was of his generative powers. I meant to deliver justice, to no longer debate using only the speech and grammar of the impostors but, on horseback, in armour, to go and free the detainee wherever he was, and to loose him of the books he composes like a prisoner forging his shackles, with inexplicable meticulousness. I saw him as the most docile editor of the grand politics of illusion disseminated by the Spanish kings and the traffickers of pearls. I saw him as a servant; I thought I would be able to depict him as one of those coxcombs who are kept in the royal courts of Europe and notably in France, who freely employ every form of derision even if the things they would mock be themselves derisory — a lunatic by the bedside of a king more stupid or inconsequential than the clown himself, a virtual chimaera half Charles VI the Demented and half Enrique the Abulic, and who would with his somersaults, his puns, his farces of word and gesture, his posturings, give coherence to an Idiot's reign, by thrashing about before the still gazes of stern consuls. I was able to consider this Peter Martyr as my brother in distress: a little Lombard trailing his books & his notebooks behind him, the underling to whom one entrusts the essential duties, as here the description of the world.

Later, I began to grow suspicious of the zeal & efficiency which the little clerk of Lombardy brought to his role, recycling so many statements, communiqués, dispatches, rare missives, and marvels, compiling it all with the gravity of a monk or a Venetian ambassador going as a spy to every court to feel out weaknesses. So great was my pity, I interpreted his absurd zeal as the reflex of a man incarcerated, one whose very life depends on his unflagging allegiance to his guardians; but my pity knows its limits, and my readings of the many *Decades* in the end taught me that Peter Martyr, far from being an idiot manipulated by others, was in full conscience one of the most subtle yet most manifest fomenters of the newly discovered lands. It suffices to appreciate from one line to the next his perpetual harping about obedience despite his pretensions to being a nonbeliever, a quibbling polymath or philologist capable of getting infinitely lost in arguments about the etymology of a single word, like calumny for instance (is it derived from *calame* as in *calamity?*). If I, whose life depends upon God granting me another day, needed a reason to write from one night to the next a *Refutation*, that reason would be the existence of Martyr d'Anghiera & his indestructible *Decades de Orbe Novo*, printed and produced with the complicity of the Crombergers of Seville, who are in the pay of the Catholic Kings, before being paid by some Grandee or other, or by the Holy Orders, or by some *nouveaux riches* wholesalers, who will rely on your indulgence to perpetuate the imposture.

I ceased to consider this Peter Martyr as the enslaved scribe of higher powers the day I realized, to my immense regret, that he is no passive page-setter, but rather at the heart of a coalition of conspirators, the most intrepid of their number, to the point of embarrassing those conspirators who would have liked to endow their fable with the uncertainty and reserve that are characteristic of true facts (a feigned tone of hesitation, as of the great man who knows how to stop talking at just the right moment so as to profit in silence from the respect his interlocutors owe him). At the heart of a ring of boastful and calculating courtiers, in his clear and harrowing voice, he will be the chattiest, he will give a speech as exacting as the inventory drawn up by a grocer convinced his counter-boy is pilfering stock. And the minor clerk-teacher-canon will not stop at taking notes on the world as it is, nor at collecting seashells from the beaches of Portugal, nor limit himself to a simple report of the facts, but he will see to it that his too widely scattered letters become the official version of the story and resemble sempiternal declarations of victory. Not a minor, duped secretary, conducted to the side of princes for a quick dash of his quill, but rather the boldest, the most boastful and vainglorious instigator, without ever quitting his writings, assigned to this post since he lacks the real courage of beggars and of sailors, or because he scents danger with his unmatchable opportunist's nose. No dupe, but a duper, and remarkable in his way, because he managed to have his pretty pages spread all over what came hence to be called the old world, all in order to stagger baronets, inn-maids, farmboys, the precious angiologists of the Vatican with their meticulously filed nails. Duper so as to not be a dupe (unless he was fooled before he came into the secrets of princes, before he began to have his part in them): with the Millennium reduced now to little more than a dry, paltry hope, rendered all the more austere by the rigour of monks, the intransigence of the Savonarolas, and the drastic hospitality of the new Inquisition, it needed this genius to invent a land where paradise and Pliny's bestiaries are yoked together for the greatest happiness of each and all.

The little canon is hardly just a humble notary clerk for what arises — he has nothing in common with those footmen who commit their masters' assets to paper, and if he was one formerly, 'twas only time enough to appraise the imposture and the profit to be drawn therefrom; in a like manner do kings, if their caprice compels them to, sometimes assign to their fools uninhabited, exotic territories, so that they can rule over them and apply to them their unusual politick (the 22nd card of the Tarot). When his time comes, Peter Martyr does not content himself to describe virgin lands and gold mines, erstwhile properties of Solomon but, by carefully measuring the outline of lands imagined by others, by describing league by league the coastlines our caravels sail up and down, by imbuing the nuggets with one of those tawny hues between red and yellow which a jeweler's jargon makes enticing, he evaluates his dowry and word by word secures a kingdom unto himself, at once a land of marvels and bankable inheritance. Thus does the little secretary, charged with the declension of substantives, discover in himself a colonist's appetite, and ever so swiftly that avidity will have to be dealt with, because it will grow restless and stamp its feet; and so the canon of Granada will be offered an imaginary country, one he can enjoy without the slightest inconvenience: he will become the abbot of an island on which, so it is said, he will never set foot. Then Peter Martyr the Immobile, the stay-at-home, the little master of bulletins and opuscules, but great Prince-Abbot regnant over a domain the size of a seal, since it exists nowhere else but on a map of the world, Peter Martyr will not find it difficult to magnify his land, as he formerly exaggerated the merits of Columbus, exaggerated the size of emeralds, the colour of parrots, and the outlandishness of monsters; it will be easy for him to affirm that his island is the most fortunate of all, because it has the advantage of depending on his description alone.

For, unlike other impostors, Peter Martyr has never taken the trouble of embarking for the west — a nice round trip of it with a dip at Cape Verde, then some idols to be carved from exotic woods upon arriving at one's destination, then come back a hero or risk drowning. While many admirals have paid for this hollow talk with their lives, including the disreputable Pinzon, who died in the care of bonesetters from a chancre contracted off the coast of Guinea, the clerk has amused himself writing, on par with his illustrious vainglory, almost a book a day (he does not fail to add: "in the quietude of my study"), which adds up to many texts, that is, many reasons for inquietude with regard to the fragility of his lies. 'Tis undoubtedly the sign of his wisdom, a vulpine wisdom, that

Peter Martyr never sets sail across the Ocean into the sunset; because he would not want to experience the void and the obscurity, because he would not wish to discover the remains of St. Brendan grounded on a reef, because he especially does not want to be marooned off the coast of the Azores with his crown of laurels for a buoy, nor to realize as he drowns that he has just been given his due.

Eulogy, dithyramb, secular hagiography are the strong suits of canon Peter Martyr, as well as a facility with speech no doubt learned in the markets of Milan; his glorifications of marvels quite often verge on chicanery, much in the way the saint's raptures oft verge on sin. Despite his efforts to merit the title of poet, Peter Martyr remains a grocer; he is like those men who do not shrink from dispensing with the crumbs of their treasures to stimulate sales, or who let their customers touch silk, inconceivable silk, for only a fleeting instant, betwixt the thumb and forefinger. It is said that along with his letters to the pope he sends little sachets of spices and seeds, of cinnamon sticks and even more exotic powders, possibly auriferous, like samples of that new world, to be savoured on the tip of one's tongue. I, who disabuse rather than bewitch, I who have the austere and doubtless futile job of celebrating nothingness and distributing it like a peddler, toting it on my shoulders, I who disenchant, I would not know how to likewise accompany my letters with such spice samples, and for very good reason, for the refutation is not tangible and has no flavour — circumspection is bland. It is said that Pope Leo X unreservedly loves the tales of adventure of the canon Martyr, with none of the restraint that his rank obliges; they even say he reads them aloud to his nieces and those women who are permitted within the walls of the Vatican by its ambiguous protocol; accordingly then, let us recognize that Peter Martyr and his *mundus novus* are ecumenical, since they entertain both ladies of easy virtue and the vicar of Christ.

Whose accessory was the little Lombard canon? maybe of Enrique the Abulic, maybe of Isabella, with Ferdinand close behind, maybe of the intellectuals of Florence, who are said to have composed the letters of Amerigo Vespucci together (their unity of tone would not be another miracle of the Seventy, but evidence that their savoir faire is entirely monolithic: a tree consisting of a single trunk without branches), perhaps from the city of Genoa, ever anxious for the memory of the Vivaldi brothers' failure to be forgotten. Maybe also an accessory to the Hebrews, the sons of Abraham and of Tubal-cain, if the invention of the new world could lend their new exodus the allure of a long journey (an adventure willingly accepted, a journey toward China's gold), or if it were the only way Cristóbal Columbus, a crudely disguised Marrano, could find to go off at the queen's expense to discover another promised land on the far side of the Canaries, to offer it to the diaspora. Backed by the Sephardic banker Santángel and Isaac Abravanel (the author of a hard-headed commentary on Creation), generously funded by Queen Isabella after she had, so they say, pawned off her pearls and diamonds to Jews in Toledo, the admiral Columbus, with the *Zohar* concealed under his shirt-front to supposedly ward off the cold, would have led five hundred of his brethren westward in the hopes of finding the ancient city of Ophir, from which in his time King Hiram imported rare timber, stone, and gold to rebuild the Temple. They make their way, not too joyfully though, for it is mainly since they are unable to return home that they dream of docking in lands more or less rich, where the sole inhabitants are starfish and Barbary figs. At worst, they expect they will find the forests and quarries Hiram exploited to build the second temple, in other words, to find a provisional refuge for the next two millennia in the hollow left by their temple, from the far side of the world, as if it had stamped its footprint there.

Some reason as follows: if the imposture of the new world has its origin in back rooms, in a network of secret men, in books at first rare, that go on to earn an editorial fortune, in a hermeneutics as patiently revealed as it was formerly patient and silent (a knowledge paradoxically transmitted from sealed lips to sealed lips, with a finger across them), if the imposture resembles a revelation reserved first to initiates, later made available to the profane, seeming to crumble and deteriorate a little in the process as it comes into contact with the air and the sweat of palms, if the imposture, finally, is a massive and cruel hope because vain, offered to men by their peers or their enemies, then perhaps the imposture is the work of the Kabbalists, presently invisible and casting no shadow because they know to lie low, or because they were repelled to the frontier, or converted with a single word into disciples of Cisneros: Christians bearing light. There is no magic that is not chalked up one day or the next to the Jews, since the Egyptians of Thoth and the Chaldean Magi Kings native to Seville are now out of the question: because they have a facility with letters and because in their exile and in that dereliction which they both extol and refuse, they have sought to dabble a little in each science, in the way every man gropes his way about in order to gauge the extent of his space, his gaol if need be, or his temporary freedom. According to a discreet but commonly held opinion, conjecture is in fact the unending place where the Hebrew disciples of Aboulafia live, more or less comfortably, more or less at home there: a domain of spectres, of spirits, of sparks of chance, of calculations and anagrams. The naked and tormented creature rolls itself up in the sheets to combat the cold, then in the folds of successive commentaries in order to cure itself of solitude.

Thus: it did not take long for the Kabbalah to be discussed in relation to the newfound continents, or for the sons of Abraham and Eleazar to be credited with the invention of a land mass where all evidence indicates there is nothing, but where evidence is brought low by talk, like the devil by holy water. That the idea of a new world should set sail from Seville the very day after the publication of the edict of expulsion, that is perhaps just one more great coincidence, the likes of which this world has seen so many of (sometimes quite amusing); but, in place of chance, the suspicious sage requires something more: relations of cause and effect. So that which has been said elsewhere, in various places, I briefly take it up in my turn, without either denying or confirming it: filled with sorrow to see their compatriots leaving in exile or humiliating themselves through conversions but still be persecuted none the less after, filled with dread to see the agents of the Holy Inquisition as incisive as ever, eager to weed out the sincere converts from the pretenders, some of the Jews decided to put forth the hope of a new world: a country without a past and without kings, where the law of the purity of blood would be no more intelligible than the exploits of Merlin. Out of fear that the edict of expulsion would scatter their population irrevocably, out of fear the faith of Moses would fade away in dilution, the rabbis preferred to reunite their nation, even at the cost of deceiving themselves, by allotting it a cape. The west would be the exact opposite of the lost orient, contemned for its perdition, it would be the only free place remaining on earth, inhabited only by such phantoms as teeming Europe no longer knows what to do with. They have chosen the sunset, a courageous but logical destination, as if a prophet had prophesied to them that God would permit them to live in the future, while leaving the past behind. So the Talmudists, the Kabbalists, the followers of Gikatilla, those of Isaac the Blind, all the heads of families have taken up old legends of lands beyond the horizon, a mixture of fables as old as the Misnah and metaphors spun by the Florentine alchemists. The Jews, again Hebrews after the time of their exile, chose Cristóbal Columbus to be their makeshift Moses, though his family name is no more Jewish than his first name (one day it will perhaps be discovered that the name *Cristóbal*, after being subjected to the logic of the Gematria, refers to the salvation of the Jews, thus situating the Promised Land on the far side of the Ocean, exactly 370 leagues to the west of Cape Verde).

The Mosaic principle of the promised land is that one does not go there, one meets one's death (one's apotheosis, one's immortality) on the way there, on an escarpment, just a stone's throw away — whereas the disciples' error is to boldly set out for it: although promised, that land must yet remain a perennial promise, always just outside the tent. I have so often travelled on the highways, I have so often marched in funeral processions, that on my last legs I was able to fancy myself the wandering Jew; and that is doubtless why I refuse to believe in an end to the exodus (this would be a false report); I refuse to believe that a promised land becomes a land of fulfillment through the enchantments of a boat ride, not just for the restless Hebrews spread out over all the continents, but for all humanity, condemned since the dawn of time to be cast out of its home.

The princes of Spain, who are allies to the expelled Hebrews, or the great families of Florence, bribed by Alexander VI: it will take these and many legions more to dream into existence islands with no known use. I would respectfully invite you to compare that multitude to the majestic solitude of Joan when she did pass as Pope John. The enterprise of Joan was realized by one, whereas the invention of the new world is the work of a great many; she basks in her role, priding herself on her ability to tell the initiated apart from the uninitiated, much as a monarch must have enemies and pronounce their names with each new season, if only for the sake of diplomacy. The ruse of Pope Joan was the ruse of one alone, concealed even from those in her innermost circle: servants, footmen, and tasseled guards whose essential duty it is to look elsewhere. Without a doubt Joan's imposture would have prevailed for longer, beyond her death even, if she had made accomplices of her servants, a confessor, then by extension the whole sacred college (all but a mute, an idiot, a senile), eventually taking half of Europe into her confidence, against the other staunchly skeptical half: because then the accomplices would have upheld the imposture for the sole pleasure of being in on the secret. Except there is every indication that Joan's fantasy, or her cruelty, consisted first of a deceit, then later a self-revelation, so that she could feel the perhaps even greater pleasure of authenticity's irruption into the ranks of the imposture and its velvety attire: right at the heart of it all.

If I had presently to praise Pope Joan, I would affirm that usurpation is properly speaking not an unjust seizure of power, but a seizure of power *tout court*, because injustice is comprised half of usurper & half of the usurped, much like fealty. There is no true usurpation but in the eyes of clerks who think that legitimacy is to be found in some book of law or birth register or a formal declaration of surrender. Imposture exists only for clerks convinced by the dreams of I know not which philosopher-prince, and who believe in an ideal government (similarly, sin has meaning only for deacons who hold the Saviour's foreskin, protected from all humidity and temptation within the Lateran Basilica, to be the repository of all the world's virtue). Apart from the attention they devote to Joan who was John, the chronicles of here and abroad tell of buffoons who became kings, with the same arrogance, the same sense of responsibility as their princes, in the absence of legitimate heirs, and seemingly with the same sadness; chronicles mention mercenary usurers and receivers of stolen goods elevated to the throne who thought they heard a people respectful of laws murmuring to them, they speak of footmen who went on to become extremely competent emperors, hard workers & good ambassadors; it can fall to the usurper to assure the continuity of the State, it can happen that the usurper, by taking the sceptre in hand, is restored to his or her rights.

I plead here for Joan and her usurpation, which was a way of recovering her rights; I plead for her by invoking what no other commentator invokes (because they are solely preoccupied with the law), I plead by invoking the solitude of the impostor, the solitude of the man-girl, the solitude of she for whom privacy reduced to so little was a necessity and the last resort of the vulnerable. I plead by invoking the chagrin of that girl who became a monk and later pope in answer to the desires of the flesh, whose desire to marry led her into a life of solitude, who in the end grew weary of consecrating her love to naught else than shadows suscitated by the scraps of candles, in her chamber designed for the use of so many old men. I invoke those feelings of rancour that the impostor may feel in spite of the success of his or her imposture, because if it is successful, over time it ceases to be a personal triumph to which others are accomplices, and instead becomes an abdication by others, of which Joan is the tributary: as a usurper, a king is more or less the depositary of a collective defeat. I invoke the sincerity of the usurper: the sincerity of her love of her métier, the sincerity of her abilities, the sincerity of her probity and of the fatigue Joan felt every evening — & even the sincerity of the stigmata she invented with the help of the most credulous doctors, to justify the use of compresses once a month. I plead in invoking the benevolence of Joan and her placid, heartfelt manner, which she turned on the farthest-flung of her flock, the crustiest pilgrims, perhaps the most taken in by her imposture, the coalmen and swineherds, who looked on her empearled crozier as a form of currency: I maintain that between this pope and her people, two mutually complicit parties, a relationship of fond amity prevails, which since knows no equivalent. (Lastly, let us recall that although Joan was a usurper, she however never sentenced Pope Marcel or Pope Lucien to the dungeon: that is all to her honour, unlike so many other impostors who stake their legitimacy on the imprisonment of every pretender to the throne.)

FOUR
The Litany of All That Gleams

You know, Sire, you on whom the sun never sets (& if it does, it does so less to obey the natural laws of the cosmos than to prostrate itself before your authority): the promoters of the new world did not originally envisage a single land situated as far away as possible, such a miracle would have been very difficult to believe. Rather, they preferred to proceed prudently by steps, spreading out so many islands like stepping stones in the Ocean, the Isle of St. Brendan, the Isles of the Hebrides, and the Fortunate Isles among others, so that they all might serve as bases to our caravels or to our imaginations, step by step, always pushing farther west.

In the way of tall tales, everyone had been content until then with the exploits of Marco, Matteo, and Niccolò Polo, who travelled to the Levant to trade their currency for legends. Those self-serving men knew how to look curious when confusion struck them dumb, when dealings slowed down, how to cast their gaze on the surrounding mountains, even to paint them indigo; they saw monsters risen out of swamps and the complex mores of somber men, bent over their spades, weather-scarred but full of a folklore beyond our ken; those men were farces at which the Polos could not laugh. In those days, the voyagers openly declared their ambitions, and set them down in official registries, left on ships, again, employing abacuses instead of sextants, which went into a panic past certain meridians, as though other stars were presiding over their course. We indulged these merchants, embarking with their utensils, returning with silk & a new description of the siren, of the Roc bird whose wing can blanket a whole city, & probably the lands of Prester John too, glimpsed to the port side, far off, in the mist and in the precipitation, the latter explaining the former. They knew how to give the kings of these countries a sufficiently credible allure for their bankers' sake, and a sufficiently fantastical allure for everyone else, who did not fear to see their goods sunk in a tempest, preferring on the contrary to listen to stories that were only a whit exaggerated, even here, at their tables, sharing their wine, with that familiarity compatriots find anew in each other's presence (preferring that magic of pure speech to the merchant's guarantees). We tolerated these voyagers, who brought back gifts for their families, tales of miracles for their neighbours, chancres for their surgeons and promises for the powerful, for the doge for example, should he want to hear stories of omnipotence. We also put up with those who left never to come back, who were swallowed up God knows where, in who knows what narrows: in a way, we relished the stories that did not return, and the silence and adventure that such vanishing implies. Then our sedentary pleasure in imagining such impeccable shipwrecks, shipwrecks having the elegance to leave the water above them perfectly smooth, without the least piece of oar or sail to stir the suspicions of whomsoever, our pleasure was a refinement, an abstraction. In dark taverns, other seamen and labourers, brawny neckless men whose heads sit squat on their trunks, pondered that nothing, that absence, speculated with little knowledge but a collective enthusiasm for the fate of those adventurers who went off never to return. And I think I can say that such besotted reasonings, of drunkards seated around a table and full of coarse convictions, are worth about as much as the arguments of Thomists on the shadows cast by angels, or regarding theophany. We speak for example of the Vivaldi brothers of Genoa, who left their father, mother, and wives behind for an Atlantic journey with India as its (putative) destination, but who never returned: from this non-return, jongleurs were inspired to pen since forgotten ditties, as well as their melodies, old women drew from them a thousand bits of gossip, two or three of which remain with us; for their part the widows have inspired a thousand elegies on the strict celibacy that scaly-skinned priests are sworn to uphold. Later still, some short tales in the manner of the *Decameron* imagined the dead man or his ghost returning to the fiancée's bedside, bringing with him the noise, the wind, the bitterness & the obscurity of tempests, of those depths where he surely lies — returning either to make love to her one last time before disappearing for good, or to grant her permission to seek in the warmer embraces of the living the thread of a life lost in waiting.

These old, naive dramas contented us no doubt, this being before the printing houses in the North had opened their doors, much more seriously: workshops now appearing all over the Empire and its outposts, then in a few other free countries as well, where they are often found adjacent to the open-pit mines and the foundries, which they sometimes resemble. For aeons, editors forever on the brink of bankruptcy flit from one infatuation to the next, from one effervescence to another, and appropriate tales of conquest by royal privilege in order to shore up their sales, & distribute to a pale public of intellectuals, enthusiasts by obligation, jealous of each other, the proofs of their curiosity: whatever it takes to satisfy that erudition that is their sole remaining dignity.

In the workshops of the Waldseemüllers notably: they round up poets drawn out of their inns and their drunkenness, whom they indulgently abandon to the delirium tremens, so that from their fevers other bestiaries may be born, which will need to be catalogued, other sirens, which will need to be situated on a map, other species of crabs out of which to make the hard-headed inhabitants of certain isles. In cabinets resembling refectories the Waldseemüllers lock in a handful of these alcoholics in the final stage of their initiation, accompanied only by one or two scribes, perfectly lucid, still as stumps, while the cheerful round get dazed, stagger about, fall down, come back to life, shouting and knocking over glasses — the scribes in bailiff's uniforms remain poised, indifferent to joy and woe alike, with their quill-tips in the margins of their papers: so they can note down if they are hearing the divagations of drunken men, to divine coherence in the disorder and relevance in what comes rushing higgledy-piggledy out of those mouths, sometimes with the froth of their own stupefying juices. Under the same roof and on a table confused with the deck of a ship, the drunkards before long persuade themselves that they are travelling on high seas, past a cape known to them alone. Sometimes nothing comes of it, sometimes descriptions of fabulous countries, but one must wait until the alcohol dilutes, and without fail undergoes a second distillation in the serpentine of their intestines, one must wait till the fury gives way to a certain phlegm, at a hair's breadth from fainting. Only at this point, when the drunken men are communing with each other in that universal love of boozers, their gazes fixed on the ceiling, do they start to invent gently sloping sand beaches by which they access unseen islands and lands of Cockaigne, where they encounter feverish and dissolute men, their peers, and ravish without the least opposition white, red, or black nude creatures whose breasts are more numerous and various than the native fruits of these regions, or than an entire flora comprised solely of petals, calyxes, and pulp of different species. Sometimes, if the alcohol is just right, and depending on the degree of fermentation, the men hard at their travails have only enough strength to imagine shipwrecks, tempests, the troughs of the waves, to justify not only their disequilibrium but ultimately their sickness, their vomiting and their drowning, the complete absence of spoils.

Other workshops (in Florence or elsewhere) labour feverishly with a stuccadore's precision, a specialist's and goldsmith's precision, a precision that is slightly cruel, as the highest talents sometimes are when they address the common people. We find cartographers there — ones who have only ever voyaged upon the surface of other cartographies, they followed their lines and off the coasts divined the presence of monsters indispensable to such voyages, from such observations they learned what form a littoral takes, how it opens to the waters of the sea or to the mouths of rivers. We find priests there, bound to reread Scripture for the thousandth time, between the lines, then between the interstices, in order to find the proof or prophecy of a *mundus novus*, the presence of new lands and of peoples different from ours, finally, if possible, a paper trail leading all the way from Galilee to the so-called West Indies: the cleverest get Jonas to wander to the Azores, and Noah, before the Flood had rendered all territories indiscernible, to journey to those incongruous archipelagoes, to rescue there the monkey, the antelope, the tiger and the parrot, to collect samples of what, at the antipodes, they say, corresponds to our fauna but for being all topsy-turvy: the inverse of a cow, the inverse of an otter. We find constant gabbers there, on other occasions authors of chivalric romances: which open with a miracle and end in wonder, and drift along from marvel to marvel, from surprise to surprise, make blazing swords to shine in the sky, set horses a-galloping, transform women into men, commence duels, play with oracles, ensure the good guys inevitably win, reserve ingenious deaths for the bad guys, suppose perfectly round islands ruled over by an all-powerful, perhaps omnivorous, or just anthropophagic eccentric for whom any shipwrecked sailor will make a good night's supper. We find defectors from Byzantium there, driven from their homes by razzias, fires, and the threat of the gallows, kept company by old iconoclasts dormant for one hundred years; we likewise find newly landed Greeks there, not angry but dazed, trading on their savoir faire, their exoticism, black olives or their libraries rescued *in extremis*: they say they want to help us discover their ancient heritage and, in the printer's studios, teach the master-printers how to make new fonts, or in an alcove or rain-proof hut they translate their classics into our languages. These Greeks enliven the workshops with their superstitions, deprecated though they are by Euhemerus, which is why our already complicated maps are newly peopled with Polyphemuses, Typhons, Medusas, Tritons, whirlwinds and flying fish, gaping mouths, reefs, and continents with varying dimensions situated wherever, in the west maybe. We find Bourguignons there, who will later be your subjects, Sire; but also, in waiting, Castilian ambassadors, an apostolic nuncio, the Venetian consul come to make his case, or play the part of spy. We find a scholar there too, wrapped up in all his pensiveness and a luxury of precautions, preceded, but just barely, by his sweet-talking reputation, a scholar come from Paris and its Universities where, with much passion and as much caprice, he took part in controversies, debates, arguments, who knows what else, going up to the rostrum, then back down from the rostrum, assuming his position, then withdrawing, swearing on his life, taking God as his witness, ridiculing his opponent before embarrassing himself, as if that in itself ensured fair treatment — and, instead of insinuating an iota between the father and son, he and his peers troubled themselves over the doctrine of the soul's immortality, he pronounced the words of the quintessence, entelechy or *insolubilia*, he settled this or that question before taking part in the debate over the three Marys, always with the same ardour. Barons are there too, military officers and diplomats come from England and Holland to get an idea of what they might resemble, these territories that a handful of men abreast of good deals divide up amongst themselves, before discussing the alloys from which their coins are cast and the state of their mines. We find artists and painters there as well, miniaturists and engravers come to pawn their talent while they wait for more honourable commissions: to try their hands, they engrave all the islands they are asked to or sketch Holy Virgins in the margins of the new world, which the geographers are later bound to transform into natives, by outfitting them with loincloths.

For, as you might suspect, in addition to the bands of poets convened in these back rooms, the discoverers also need a great many competent artists: the artists will know how to paint landscapes from whatever whimsical descriptions they are given, and they will add their grain of salt too, in the details, will know just how to add a fringe to the natives' costumes — those strange little touches will be the mark of their talent, their unique signature. The greatest names of Tuscany have for the most part refused to stoop to such drudgery; the colourists of Venice, excluded from the plot, could not be approached. All that were left were the minor masters and the least inept disciples, the pieceworkers kept on by the country nobles, or those whom fate elects time and time again to paint Saint Marthas in the dark recesses of chapels. It's for this reason that the agents in charge of spreading the idea of the new world sought out an original by the name of Piero, and dragged him out of his hovel for a moment, so that he might see in broad daylight what the sun looks like, and henceforth humanity. In Florence, this second-rate painter, who they say lives off of hard-boiled eggs and in mortal fear of thunderstorms, remains famous for having, at the ripe age of twenty, designed funeral chariots and the costume of Death escorted by skulls and bells, during carnival time. In a young man, such a presumptuous knowledge, not of death, but of death's trappings, surely contributes to his reputation as both a visionary and a clown. He did not stop at painting his danse macabre, abusing the colour black, but these cadavers and these gallows, these open-work puppets, hung from their necks, he gave form and made them file through the city, to the sound of the hurdy-gurdy. And that is why, when the back rooms of Florence were recruiting painters, some of the agitators, notably the members of the Vespucci tribe, thought of Piero, who was ignored by everyone else and by his own, abandoned by his disciples, shunned by his masters, visited less and less by his patrons, thenceforth holed up in his ever sealed, ever somber chamber, with nary a visitor. I presume that his particular talent, especially when it takes as its subject fabulous beasts, the tails of slow-worms, Leviathans, the Styx, journeys to Cythera, or the Apocalypse, his talent but also his hotspur arrogance, his lack of scruples, his deftness in dealing with the Medicis and their enemies, his urgent need of finances, that farcical cynicism solitary people contract once they have made up their mind about humanity and shuttered their windows, I assume that all of these things constitute the qualities of a painter, portraitist, and landscape artist who is engaged in secret services. I do not designate this Piero casually, and it is not without proof that I declare him to be an accomplice to the imposture: I know what connexions he has to Pope Alexander Borgia and to his son Valentino, and I can well surmise how that poorly licked bear, despite his airs to being another Anthony covered with sand and scorpions, weaves through the halls of princes with a spy's ease when the situation requires it, at the Lateran and in Florence both. All that we have said of the blackness of his dirge, an intransigent grime since it rose up to the ceiling and paraded itself through the chic streets, shews compatible with the fact that Piero used to frequent the great families of the city, apart from the Vespuccis of whom we have already said a word, the Strozzis, and the Del Puglieses — leaving at the residence of each of these his distinctive touch.

For Piero, to paint the new world's portrait took more than simply plagiarizing his own *Origine du monde*, by inverting the curvature of palms, deforming coastlines, and defying all immediate interpretation. He also had to invent new varieties of flowers petal by petal, new birds feather by feather, and to redefine the navels of men after those of women, so as to give rise to surprise and credulity at once, and to lift the fauna and flora from Pliny's stories about the Gorgades Islands, Pomponius's stories of the Cassiterides Islands, the Germans' bits of gossip about the Seawaifs, who are most surely sirens, or, alternatively, concerning Wasserjungfern, whose breasts, God knows, defy all comprehension. I have never laid eyes on it, but the portrait that he did of Mademoiselle Vespucci has been described to me in great detail: the motif of the shawl in which the young girl is wrapped is exactly the one that Amerigo the brother (or the cousin?) describes in one of his *Letters*, reputedly sent from the Indies. (Of his series of the new world, only quick sketches are exhibited, done in that attractive style of which Florence is so fond, while the paintings themselves remain elusive: rolled and bound, sealed like an ambassador's pouch or the plans for a military campaign, they are probably gathering dust today in the vaults of some bank.)

Images no longer sufficing, it was necessary to present the masses with a more palpable form of evidence (one has to deal with starving wretches who refuse to eat bills of exchange). Some fruits? Portugal grows enough of those in Madeira; winds from elsewhere? the Portuguese find those in the Azores. As for the traffic in gold powder, which is traded for pieces of glass, it has long served to justify the presence of the Portuguese in the heart of Mandingo territory; as early as fifty years ago, Diego Gómez brought back without ostentation almost 180 pounds of gold, which he had the sagacity to brandish before the noses of his sovereigns. In our day, to prove the existence of undiscovered lands, tinpot sailors, after having gone off to Cape Verde to sow their wild oats, remove from their pockets or their coffers sackfuls of imperfect nuggets, mixed with sand, which they exhibit to the people standing about on the quays, before exhibiting them to monarchs, Isabella and her court, though they have seen that many times before, and if not sackfuls of tough, coal-like nuggets, then partially melted bullions, traditional jewelry curiously resembling that from the island of Djerba, or pieces of fabric which seem to come from the Tyrrhenian coast, or such garments as Herodotus describes in detail in the pages of his *Researches*.

Yet such evidences are necessary and, so it seems, expected: that gold, which the people will never touch, except with their eyes, having to settle for its likeness without even taking the time to distinguish the real from the fake, that gold is the most manifest token of the new world. You would think that these men got bagfuls of gold for their cozenage, when in fact, once the procession of Wise Men is over, the nuggets will go back into the coffers of Isabella and disappear for good, while they come back to us, satisfied, their pockets empty, a little stunned though, which is to say, convinced, because they saw the treasure-pieces passed fleetingly before their eyes — and in turn these converts will convince their families. But these tokens, these spoils which the spectators applaud before going home, which are at once empty and full, will appear meager to an accountant's eyes; it only counts as currency when it is before the noses of inattentive, easily lulled noddypeaks, whether they be fishermen from Lisbon or an archbishop Isabella keeps under her boot. Some stagecraft is necessary, and especially the complacency of the dupes themselves, in order to transform something so paltry into a new world treasure.

A different kind of complacency is required on the part of the Catholic Kings, the Spanish Grandees, the master of Alcántara, scholars like Nebrija, whose brain is befogged by grammar, and sundry other notables yet renowned for their judgements, all of whom are required to act as though they were unaware that these few grams of silver and gold are taken out of Castile's coffers, on order of the queen, packed up by night on ships, and leave our shores, only to come back six months later, after having made a few rounds on the open sea, exactly in the manner of a beginner at sailing school who tacks back and forth a few times before returning to port.

Pitiful tokens *&* proofs, and nothing new under the sun, when we recall the profitable trade taking place between the Bakhoy and the Falémé on the great African continent, when we recall the merchants' accounts of those majestic, silent ceremonies during which the Portuguese on one side, the negrœs on the other, each set their goods down without a word, adding some, removing some, till both parties were satisfied. The gewgaws allegedly brought back from the useless isles pale in comparison to the riches that the exploiters of mines and Moorish caravaneers haggle over, they look scant indeed when placed alongside the cargo that seven hundred camels transport from Timbuktu to Tunis; and that gold powder transported to Seville and conspicuously unloaded on its docks, as though it were the embalmed index finger of St. Peter, calls to mind the cockles of James the Great that the pilgrims en route to Compostela buy near Montauban, from unscrupulous dealers, when they cease to wish to go on any farther.

Pretty much anything is available in the ports of the Maghreb, in Tunis but also in Homein where gold powder and ingots are melted down in the marketplaces to be bought and resold, to say nothing of ivory from Sofala, iron from Zanzibar, salt from the different kingdoms of Barbary, with which Seville has ties dating back several centuries.

One of the lessons that I for my part would like to import from the other shore, to depose it at your august feet, concerns the natives exhibited in Spain, outfitted with feathers and ochre or indigo-shaded loincloths, who parade around carrying the cross but pray to their own god (a sort of Ishtar figure dressed up as a rooster). They are depicted as a substitute for coffers overbrimming with gold, that gold forever promised to the morrow; they waddle about before your crowns while taking care to seem terrified &, it's said, they open the festivities in Seville in the same way that a young bride opens the ball. They are known as "new men," and soldiers ensure that their posture is bent so that they seem to have crossed a great many oceans, weathered sundry tempests, suffered hunger and thirst. Because they speak only gibberish, they are held up as proof of the existence of another territory; as for their fright, it would serve as evidence that their bodies do indeed contain souls. We present these red-skinned natives to the court, and each pretends to retain hardly any memory of Nuño Tristão & Antonio Gonçalves, who brought back from Africa, a long time ago already (under the reign of King John II), men of a reddish complexion, so red that they were said to be covered in ferruginous soil; and me who amasses my memories into a heap of so many twigs and feathers, I resuscitate the figure of Diego Gómez, who returned from the island of Tidra after commandeering twenty-three of these rubicund, frightened men, promised to a rare and exciting future. Old, bookish men, who have no incentive to lie, knowing that they stand to gain nothing from this new world before they die, tell of six hundred or six hundred and fifty of these reddish individuals, known as Cenegii, brought to Algarve, made to kneel, their jaws lashed with straps. In truth, where these wondrous exiles come from is: the coasts of Africa exploited by Portugal; that is where those nude girls originate, surrounded by thoughtfulness and a curiosity that binds them: the colonies of King Alfonso. They are Guanches from the Canaries and not marvels from suddenly surfaced islands; they are Caucasian women or virgins from Guinea, sold by the lot against some maravedís.

In our day, in the Canaries, in Madeira, priests are saving the griots from slavery if they can manage to dunk them in holy water. Meanwhile, in the New Indies (in truth on the African continent), captures are being made with a tenfold efficacy, because progress is now the rage. But, before the men and women are brought to our cities, we dress them up in shirts inspired by Hungarian folklore, we adorn them with jewels from Old Galicia and even, they say, some retailers file their teeth in order to give them that incisiveness proper to man-eaters. On the other hand, we would not dare present the lords of Castile with convoys of Amazons, who are ever ready to ask men, if they wish to ride on horseback, to consent to such sacrifices as the women made when they chose to become archers. (Evidence seems to indicate these women never existed; however, Gaspar de Carvajal claimed to have seen some of them, scores in fact, although he lost an eye en route: perhaps this explains it.)

The study of imposture requires us to review some celebrities who, whether by sheer willpower or by accident, narrowly landed their names in the history books, to say nothing of the geography books. Columbus? an old mumpsimus inflated by Isabella, who has the breath of a creator-god by virtue of her outsize ambitions; and, in fact, this sailor on every sea and from every country, like Cæsar, who is said to have been a husband to all women & a wife to all men, is endowed in his portraits with a plump and fulsome allure, making us think him full of those breezes on which are nourished who knows what fabulous beasts of the Orient. He also has a round face on whose surface the early signs of rosacea announce themselves according to Ptolemy's rules of projection (later adopted by Fra Mauro), & eyes divided between disgust & avidity. Among the handful of men chosen to act out the discovery, he is undoubtedly the most pathetic, whereas by comparison Vespucci looks as sly as an usurer and the Pinzón brothers too perfectly like the eternal couple of symmetrical, charlatan twins described in adventure stories. Despite his bourgeois immovability, Columbus had something of a jostled, unstable quality, as if struck in advance by reefs, or thrown off plumb by the listing of his barges.

I have seen, Sire, the remains of those nutshells that we are assured did cross the Ocean to the new lands: I saw there only sorry mizzenmasts, holes of ship-worms and inferior pitch, my incompetence in matters of navigation notwithstanding. But I do credit the inventors of the new world with a certain honesty in the usage of the imposture though, for having the courage to deliver up both the enigma and its key to the sagacity of the non-believers: thus, to have given the three marvellous boats destined for such high praise the names of petty prostitutes, *The Painted One, The Street Girl, The Mary-Lie-Down-Here*, is tantamount to playing with an open hand and deceiving us, without actually telling a lie.

Admiral Columbus stands at the bow, fluctuant, disheveled; he believes that by more tightly gripping his crucifix he maintains his sense of balance. Meek as his demeanor seems, I cannot distinguish the face of the believer from that of the gullible mark, nor can I separate his Christian countenance from his superstitious profile; I imagine him with his hands and arms encumbered with a Bible he does not read, a never-opened copy of Augustine, and a map of the seas, the decipherment of which he confides to an apprentice. The inventors ultimately decided to present to the henceforth old world this Pulcinella alternating betwixt moments of cowardice and fits of rage, though there were thousands of other unemployed sailors to choose from, all ready to leave the scene of their latest crime and to arrive at the scene of their next one, and thus go round the world, filling full their bustling lives.

In the taverns of sailors and opportunists, the aforenamed Columbus must have held office as a regular, though he did not hesitate long before rebaptizing himself Colón, since the use of an alias is the way of crooks and fugitives, and names have on simple men the effect of spells (in lieu of *Cristóbal* he prefers to sign *Christo Ferrens* the better to entice all those Dominicans soon lost in the sea, lost in their horizon, dissolved in that yearning for the west). And this Columbus, on whom the eagle of destiny alights, is one of those pirates who have tasted a little bit of everything at everyone's expense, and concluded after betrayal upon betrayal that the mixed flavours of existence do not leave the tongue bitter, but neutral, absolutely, as though stripped of scruples and of judgement, from having tried everything. They had good reason, the scoffers, to scoff just before they gave in and admitted this new world, for it is so mild a thing to admit. They must have had good reason too to call this Cristóbal the *Admiral of Mosquitœs*, owing to his face, which resembles a swollen squash, or because in his day, along the coasts of Africa infested with parasites, he knew their torments. Perhaps they had occasion, before retracting the title, to baptize Cristóbal *the pirate*, while others in the streets of Seville, as spiteful as they were sincere, called him *le fallador* because of his numerous lies.

For my part, Sire, I would like to humbly remind you, without fear of delivering a brave, strapping fellow up to your justice since divine justice already fixed his sentence some years back, that in his time he served in every army, and was like all good pirates a pistoleer or swordsman in the company of the bandit Cazenova (himself in the employ of King Louis XI of France). He is available to the first to arrive on the scene then, to the grandiose if they be grandiose, to the ordinary if they be ordinary, we can suppose him allied to the expedient or the universal depending on the salaries each of these, as Fate, can pay him, or at least promise to pay him. He responds to the recruiters like sinfulness responding to temptation, taking the lead sometimes, and shewing an eagerness that had to be held back by crises. We see him drafting his curriculum vitæ on the fly while others, sitting across from him, draw up a contract on an inn's tablecloth, and nudge their neighbour for a signature. This naive and rubicund Columbus lets himself get carried away because that's his job, and swears before Isabella, as readily as before a pair of obliging and magnanimous drunks, no strangers to rodomontades since they are their sad lot in life and they share them constantly, avers with the derision of a ninny going before half the world's kings that he has navigated on every sea, known Thule at the extreme north and set foot on frozen seas, and circumnavigated Africa too (a voyage hitherto effected only by Portuguese sailors) in order to reach the western shore of the Indies and bring back more mace, more cinnamon, more cloves than ever before. These are but lies, they contribute to his reputation, which he oversees with the help of ship-lords tasked with devising from inception to conclusion not just the expedition, but also the world waiting to be discovered. Many conflicting or supporting legends were circulated before, during, and after his voyages, like that of the egg made to stand on end, a feat attributed, as everyone knows, to Brunelleschi alone — so let us give credit to the truly clever: to architects, if they be architects. On the faith of certain witnesses and grudge-bearers, it is said that, sword in hand, he happened to attack his own compatriots or the master who had given him his pay only the day before.

Surely it was to flatter the Genoans that the Catholic Kings invented this big boy, of the kind who, *ad vitam aeternam*, shall remain altar boys, whether they are consorting with sailors, standing at the gunwale, or betwixt the thighs of courtesans: whilst he was boosting Seville's profits, Christopher Columbus had the merit to make Genoa fashionable.

I have already explained at great length, Sire, how the Kabbalists, according to certain witnesses, saw in the figure of the admiral a new guide who would lead them safe and sound, far from Pharaoh, by parting the waters. But, surely, you will recognize that he is not some famous Moses, this Columbus with the face of a pastry-cook and the lifestyle of a sailor hardly bettered by confession; he is not some passion-filled Moses, because, of that great Hebrew patriarch, he has managed to retain only the stuttering. The witnesses saw heading toward the horizon, floating askew, a sort of Noah's ark, cram-full of couples and silverware (Spain, your Spain, will regret those taxpayers' absence for many years to come: they paid the *servicio y medio servicio* on the nail): enough silver to scuttle with dignity — the dignity of men who know themselves already dead.

While we are on the subject of sham sailors, now or never we ought to evoke Vespucci, that other audacious player (especially when it's other people's money on the line). Vespucci? All Florence's trickery, all that city's savoir faire in matters of politics & of finance, of art and of colour: a mix of æsthetics & of strategy equally at work in the ballets of court. A forked, angular man, good for blocking the wind, but in a most specific way, contrary to his rival Cristóbal, whose complexion is spherical, equal by nature in all directions, and therefore insusceptible to the most subtle changes of course. For the divulgaters of the new world who seek to imbue their fables with rhythm and surprise, this Vespucci of good family, this manager of the Medicis' fortune, this Mercury of promissory notes is by contrast the necessary adversary of the commoner Columbus, hero to plasterers, steeped in devotion, moon-swallowing, as avid as the poor: with a fury that anticipates his failure, and the destitution to come. Cristóbal is trading, pecuniary ambition, petty profits, tinpot marvels to be fobbed off in the streets of Saragossa and, if he does happen to find paradise, let it at least be one where he can scrape copper and plant spelt. Whereas Vespucci is art for art's sake, theorized from the comfort of silk sheets by a rich man's son. Less approachable, more arrogant, more keen, this young man was also the more difficult to domesticate, and once he gets momentum, he might not be content to only discover land and play the administrator's role, he might attempt to usurp God in His role then, since God both creates and lays claim to continents by a single word, on the faith of a single utterance.

One common point unites them: the letters of Vespucci were composed, we know, by a group of poets, in Florence, no doubt since it is far easier to write on land than whilst rocking in a boat at sea. As for Cristóbal Columbus' famous letter addressed to Santángel, there's no doubt that Santángel was responsible for its every word, and that he took care to make a clean copy of it before affixing his seal thereto.

Tidings reach me also of a certain Fernando Cortés, and I have seen his face in a portrait, which strikes me as being at once that of a vigorous Greek and of a bearded hotspur; his face is leonine, his eyes a pair of juniper berries. He was painted from hearsay in that posture of Poseidon, half in the Ocean, half out, with his hand probably resting on a globe whereon the new world imposture is bursting into relief, like knobs of the pox on a sick man's pate. He is a great adventurer, too, who would make the leap from here over to the new islands as others take a ferry across the Guadalquivir. That, they assure us, is exactly the kind of lord we will have to put up with from now on, subjugated as we are at once by paradises painted on blocks of wood, by their sumptuous vegetation dwarfing all sense of human scale, and by these men of a superior caliber, who sport soldier's gorgets and are treated with as much respect as our ambassadors yesterday were, soon consuls themselves, if only by so many of the rod's blows. That is exactly the kind of lord that awaits us on the other side of the ocean: foremost a strong bellower, a sabre-rattler, a kidnapper of virgins and swashbuckler serenading under windows at dawn, who goes by *sailing large* or *with a tailwind*, and does not hesitate if his conscience tells him to (yet the heart always told him to) *luff into the breeze* (I cannot say whether these terms afflict or amuse me). First we see him slicing a suckling-pig in half length-wise; next, and with a similar technique, he takes a seat at the legislator's table, puts on a judge's wig and states the law, or dictates it, or enforces it, and consigns the proceedings, sets boundaries, calls for order, evokes morality and calls for God to come sit on his shoulder, but mistakes the dove for a pigeon and the pigeon for one of those parrots with which sailors bedizen themselves. Our lords more than ever will be these soldiers, entrepreneurs, elected because they survived, chosen because they are hotspurs, effective with their arms in hand when it comes time to put down a mutiny without worrying over the details; all also effective, it seems, but with countless parleys, when it comes time to penetrate the subtleties of law, before leading the world as if it were a voluntarily complex chaconne.

But this Cortés, I picture him to myself thus: head of the gang and lily-livered, at once an adamant contrarian and a precocious child, at least in so far as the legends spun in the bureaus mention him. If this Hernán with the allure of Neptune, but royally endowed as Pan was or as was the son of Dionysos and Aphrodite, is the model for the entrepreneurs en route toward the new world to bring back satisfaction, then we must admit that our heroes both travel there and simultaneously do not travel there, sign up and then flee, because I recall that our man, on the eve of his departure (when the ship's crew is getting ready to up anchor to take a cargo of overjoyed wretches out to the Azores to be drowned), during a romp with a *doña*, visits the Seven Cities, discovers the Hidden Isle, then begins to buck as all men do at one time or another, later or sooner, then startles at the approach of the husband, goes to run, gets his legs caught in his sword, trips, but instead of staying to fight, slips out the window and flees on one foot, because he broke the other. Thus, while Cortés hobbles along and goes into hiding for two years during his time of misfortune, a ship is sailing off to conquer the unconquered yet once again. What to say of these legends that send male heroes off to invented lands while in the meantime keeping them here, with feints as old as the world, have them playing the part of an inferior Plautus at home and over there some new Titanomachies?

Because I know, from having listened to those who knew him closely, that this Cortés corrupted by Alcántara was on this side of the world no more than a *doña*'s man, sliding from one bed to the next, and with surely better knowledge, from having explored them, of the sloping of a woman's contours than the sloping of the depths of the approaching Canaries, or the profile of Madeira. But I am not here, Sire, to once again compare the female body to desert islands; I do not wish to recycle old tropes; I have no love for restuffers: just know that, with great sympathy, I use the very words that a Cortés would not hesitate to use, were he here in person.

The least credulous witness because the most isolated (kept to a certain reclusion, which is, by superfluity, that of the hermit, the melancholic, the political prisoner, or the celibate), motivated solely by extreme prudence and won over by the gravity of mourning, even if he does come to see farce everywhere around him, cannot but admit that the imaginary lands where goat-men & one-breasted women frolic about inspire covetousness. This would just be more of the same if it were only a question of gold pieces traded for promises, bushels of wheat exchanged for some good stories, but the situation waxes more serious when crowned heads, weary of duping others, decide to dupe themselves, as if they sought to restore justice by sharing. Then the great dukes get carried away in the game and, with all the formal protocol of nobility, argue over the rights to own islands that are probably every bit as fanciful as the back of the Leviathan, where St. Brendan went aground. That is probably what the least gullible find most unnerving and what ultimately does in their certainty: they durst not think that the papal bulls and treaties signed in high pomp have their basis in dust; they durst not imagine that the whole Vatican apparatus trailing secretaries and archbishops in its wake has for its founding axiom naught else than a sailor's pleasantry and for its objective only a procession through Seville of Blacks disguised as birds. King Don Afonso, well before these useless islands became famous, had already conceded to the knight Joham Voguado the rights to any lands, any whatsoever, that might be discovered to the west; before that Isabella, duchess of Bourgogne, had obtained from this same

Afonso the concession of certain small islands of the Azores where she had ordered nearly two thousand of her compatriots to be dispersed, like hares into a meadow. And similarly Don Enrique managed to extract from the king, for the Order of Alcántara, spiritual jurisdiction over any lands to be discovered; next, so as not to be late, Henry VII hastily accorded to his appointed navigator Cabot the right to discover new lands, more to the north but westerly still (since the east, at those latitudes, is but an ice-skating rink reserved for Russia's tsars). And I have not mentioned the bull of Adrian VI, entitled *Omnimodo*, which accords to the Franciscans (to each his client) some rather obscure privileges concerning their mission, nor have I mentioned the bulls of Alexander VI, *Inter Cætera* and *Eximiæ Devotionis*, finally *Dudum Siquidem*, which is said to have been postdated, which is no sin for God, though it might be for his vicar. To the observer, these textual games and universal decrees sitting alongside and contradicting one another, these privileges to a single treasure granted to so many, these supposedly definitive treaties that are deprecated before the year is even up, that manner of signing at just two streets' remove a couple of decrees that mutually refute one another, all the while perceiving that the world carries on under the weight of such numerous paradoxes, to the solitary witness all of this looks as much like naiveté, as much like a superior ruse. Because to adopt a proprietary attitude towards invisible islands is either a proof of blindness, become lately a fashion of the courts & palaces, or it is a deliberate strategy, dictated by the crafty to the envious; to delude the people, it would hence be a question of acting as though the chimerical continents were so valuable they were worth the price of humiliations on their behalf, worth the aristocrats sharing trading posts and territories, like barkers sharing stalls in the marketplace.

All who know me, Sire, know that I have nothing of the colonist about me: I have no sense of direction, I hardly know the use of a shovel, and I am not comfortable giving orders. For some, maybe, the temptation to rule over a few acres of soil is great, to play consuls. Let us suppose for a moment that I become the proprietor of a square inch of arable land: I choose my kingdom by randomly setting down my finger on the map of the sea *Orbis Typus Universalis* printed somewhere in Moselle; I become a master of slaves, a big-time farmer, a discoverer of gold and rhubarb; I construct pyramids of sweet oranges taller than I am, then I order a farm to be built, and next to that farm, a chapel. I become a builder of cities, I found a university to rival that of Alcalá, where I dispute Averroes, I confront Ptolemy and Mandeville. I consider Seville and even Constantinople as two villages full of jackasses; I come to despise the old world, and I talk about it in so convoluted a way that my students begin to doubt its existence. Here or there, well-informed persons will say that Rome is the name of a minor god in the pagan pantheon, or that of a plant, or that of a chimaera, possessing a head but only one eye, on the nape of the neck.

FIVE
The Catalogue of Spoils

My omnipotent, tenacious, and presumptive prince, understand this, before going any further: the invention in certain back rooms of a new world that I wish to locate more precisely (a world where new trees and immeasurable grasses grow, populated by ducks with pig's heads and imperfect sirens) would mean above all else designating the world we live in as the old world. Thus do these newly emerged lands, plotted on this side of the world, in the workshops of Isabella or the Bourguignons, aspire to render our continent odious, and ultimately unbearable, populated as it is since time immemorial by beggars, by thieves, administered by them in company with other managers and tenants who are robbers, horse-traders, pimps, scrape-pennies, fake priests who swore devotion to Madeleine after having seen one or the other of her miraculous breasts in a dream, judges deaf to misery, merchants meanly measuring their phials, school headmasters, cardinals burned at the Gates of Hell, renouncing their search for holiness, opting instead for the prelacy: in short, the whole litany of miscreants (a litany known to us all, which grows the more familiar with every passing year). There would be no other reason to postulate a new world than to render ours contemptible by comparison, and to incite us to flee from it, like a bunch of capuchin monkeys driven to leap off a burning raft, thereby drowning themselves, never to be heard of ever again, neither the monkeys, nor the rotting planks. (After the departure of the last aspirants, embarked for the other world, all this country will have left will be its terminal denizens, those who hold fast, inspired by the avarice of the tick, and stand their ground: not always the best companions, but for sure the most sedentary. In effect, the thieves leave, return, while the more timorous remain behind: the collectors of spoils have a nice cruise, the receivers hold down the fort.)

The principal reason for the invention of the new world would surely be to send off into the ocean a portion of our great surplus of useless men, who fill our countrysides, our cities, and betwixt the twain our faubourgs, with the speed of a spreading plague. There are wretches, fake club-foots & sham seal-men, there are shirkers, sons-of-nobody who lost their last tooth in the course of a brawl or munching pebbles out of the riverbed, there are defrocked soldiers, so much the more to be feared, who do not only recount their exploits around a table but reenact them, through mime, swinging scraps of wood that are far more dangerous than actual swords, you can believe me, I know this from experience. The new world and the enticing advertisements which speak of it so fantastically invite all these beggars & jobless, worthless players to board dinghies, strap a sail to their torso and head due west, without demerit. A steady stream of disfigured men, ugsome-faced knaves and scrawny blackguards have thus quit terra firma, this world for its beyond, in prestigious and ruined galleons.

To get rid of these undesirables, right in the middle of the Ocean which separates our world from the countries of legend, by promising them a fortune (precious metals for some, a few acres of free land for others); to get rid of cumbersome priests, soldiers-for-hire struggling against penury, successful after seven or eight rounds; to get rid of the Spanish Grandees, snoopers or upstarts, who hang around your palaces like so many flags staked in a conquered land; to get rid of courtiers who do too much of the same; to get rid of that Someone or Other, a cavilling confessor, or a master of the Holy Office if he looks at you crosswise. Germany is digging salt mines in Carinthia in which to bury its *personæ non gratæ*; while Spain, ever more subtle, precious, *&* tawdry, more malicious too, opens its yonder gold mines and instead of excommunicating its undesirables, invites them on a voyage, wishes them a nice stay, with the devil.

What those voyages really are is: shipwrecks, journeys effected for nothing on sloops condemned ages ago, like those three nutshells Spain requisitioned from a handful of defeated men in guise of payment for their debts, journeys interrupted by drowning. We see generations of peasants leaving the country to find work in the city, next begging alms, running after old cocks or from the police, following the chapters of the low-life novel one by one before embarking on caravels. They do a quick stint (on the docks of Seville, in the sawmills of Leiria), then are sent as far away as possible, to go and see the golden apples of Hesperides and the fountain of youth, the mines of King Solomon; but once they are over the horizon, out of sight of the last remaining witnesses (the fanatics no doubt, who sleep poorly), the boats change course, they stop going west and head south, bypass the doldrums and follow the route Diego Cão took toward Namibia — or they head straight to the Canaries to unload there a labour force that is all the more efficient for not having any choice, which feeds itself on whatever it may find, and leads with heads hanging low such lives as *despendurados* must lead. And if not toward the south, then toward the north, to intermingle the paupers of Estremadura with the paupers of Ireland, make them share straw *&* hay; and if not toward the north, then by the depths, because it is easy to sink a boat, far from seeing eyes and hearts, it suffices most of the time to let the old vessel go according to its nature.

If it were within my rights, Your Highness, to improvise a teleology of disenchantment, I would say it is the destiny of every ship to perish by drowning, and to merge with the ocean floor; its job is to reach in the abysses the sand plains peopled by monsters, then, once shellfish have entirely taken them over, to regain oblivion. We invite all sorts of undesirables to come along for the voyage and discovery, including those Franciscans persuaded of having for their vocation the defence of the people of Africa: these Fathers are all too happy then to profit from the fine weather on the bridges of caravels, their capes flapping in the wind, the only ones not aware that at the indicated hour they will be tossed overboard, as one does with pieces of exotic wood to shuttle them to the mouths of rivers, toward the great cities.

The genius of the fomenters and town criers is to have imagined the existence of a buried treasure, requiring patience, clearly, but also some grueling shovel-work, it is also and especially to have set in motion this merry-go-round of departures and returns, more intoxicating perhaps than the gold that lies buried beneath the mountains of that imaginary country. Because deep down the passion of these caitiffs, so weary of their thieving, of waiting, of milking always the same old goat before going on down the road to see if the recompence is any better, is to believe themselves finally capable of leaving this world behind: and many of them, for the sole pleasure of being so poor so far from home, would pay dearly for the honour of being led off in a boat to their own perdition. (We see them everywhere, in the marketplaces, from Saragossa to Padua, at all the fairs, these talented barkers, who aren't selling ropes for their buyers to hang themselves with, but singing the praises of a new continent. Their costume is simultaneously that of the army recruiter and that of the astrologist, studded in stars from crown to toe; they know just how to make the red herrings sparkle; they employ the terms of usurers as they flip them over like a glove in order to get your last shillings; they distribute to volunteers, up and down the loading docks, notices and deeds on loose paper, worth nothing but signed by some Prince Consort or other; they wish the voyagers *bon voyage* with a wink; they round up herds of orphans, good-for-nothings, sometimes widows, and incite them to reproduce on the fallow lands, peopled at present with wild geese.)

The sponsors know what to expect, what hazardous gulfs await them just over the horizon, what cyclones swirl in a sense opposite to our own there, just as Theopompus suggests in one of his tracts, if I recall. They know that the stouthearted adventurers must scuttle their ships off the coast of the Azores if they want to give birth to legends that will go on living in this old world. Moreover, if they find it consoling to sacrifice our choicest men, sometimes even the women who accompany them, valiant court girls who retain a little of that countrified nobility and the sense of protocol against the swell of the sea, they are none the less reluctant to imperil their beautiful ships, and think it little glorious to embellish the sea floor with strange and rare buildings — even *La Santa María* met that old tub's fate, and failed to weather the trip to Cape Verde and back.

According to Isidore of Seville, the sirens are women of easy virtue; those whom they bewitch invent tales of shipwrecks afterwards to save face, and justify their delay without having to admit to having lost their bearings between shoals of sluts. In our day, it's the opposite which happens: those who have been in shipwrecks say they have mingled with sirens, their upper as well as their lower parts (quickwork, topsides) and that which, betwixt the two, joins them in the breach, because the cæsura varies per the reports, per its reckoning.

To drown a mangy dog by tossing his bone into the sea is no great feat, as you surely know. That Hernán Cortés, of whom I have spoken to you before at length, is of the de Monroy family, through his grandmother or his great-grandmother, and by this right he is an agent of the Order of Alcántara. My prince, keep this belonging in mind whenever someone would dazzle you by repeating the exploits of the *mundus novus* whilst shaking a fan at you. Also, do not forget that Isabella the furious, Isabella the tempestuous, did make Nicolás de Ovando the governor of the overseas Territories during her reign; do not forget that this Nicolás de Ovando was by virtue of his title of commander at Lares a member of the Order of Alcántara as well, & that this burlesque order, excessively pious but responsible, not content to just kiss hallowed relics, managed over the years to amass a considerable patrimony with the consent of the king & queen, your parents. (I speak not only of the territories acquired through acts of war against the infidels, however non-negligible, I refer not only to the rents received for justice done, but also to the advantage which the members of the Order, being simultaneously priests and soldiers, would have over a queen, however vigorous she might be.) If you recall finally that a grand master of Alcántara, Alonso de Monroy, was an ally to the Portuguese enemy during the wars from which Isabella emerged triumphant, but that it was nevertheless to his order that the queen confided the government of the so-called new world, then we are led to wonder what sort of schemers govern from within our palaces and churches, what sort of negotiations go on between the mercenaries and the Catholic Kings, what outrageous sums you must pay to line their pockets withal or what manner of penitent angel one must imitate in order to obtain such pardons & such handsome pensions.

But if, as I am trying to prove, these lands are nothing other than a mirage, then the government of the new world offered to Nicolás would be none other than a way of throwing him into the sea, a way to drown him so as to regain control of an order grown as wealthy as it is turbulent. You can see how each of these hypotheses supposes a Nicolás as soon duped and lost at sea, as soon a king and accomplice to the great Isabella: that is the whole history of this imposture, which has effectively blurred, & for a very long time now, the difference between dupers and dupes.

In other words: what if the invention of that new world and, by extension, the awarding of magnificent titles in distant lands, were the result of a thoroughly local quarrel here (because everything happens *here* strictly speaking) between the supporters of Gómez de Solis and the brotherhood of Alonso de Monroy, who ferociously fought each other for the control of the Order of Alcántara? In that case, the new world would be a diversion, a manœuvre orchestrated for reasons long familiar to all, to lose on the high sea young adventurers without pasts, who believe they see their destiny in the west (and among these youths are the supporters of Gómez) — or rather the new world would be the most exquisite of honorific titles, a kind of majestic bauble, that a Prince ever dreamed up to divert his vassals or insufferable pretenders with: you will be a king over there, or viceroy, what's the difference. You will be viceroy: at the antipodes with a fistful of algae in the guise of a crown, or without even leaving Spain, by settling for promised glory and such boastfulness as runs wild in the streets of Seville.

On the high seas, the lackeys have as their mission to see to the great splashes; but when they are inland, sitting near the heads of government, they prefer to carry out their schemes with the help of official documents. That's how enemy friars eliminate one another: they charter ships or they name one another viceroys in the Indies; it is also possible to have recourse to another expedient, one that has very efficiently come to replace our old powders of succession: by which I mean, the grand pox. Because someone thought it was a good idea to have a new disease be imported from the discovered lands: as if we had not already enough plagues to keep us occupied and to fill our communal pits, to make the priests quake at their pulpits, still reeling from the vibrations of the death's knell they last sounded, to make doctors dash hither and thither disguised as ravens betwixt charnel houses where there is nothing to be done but administer last rites, & above all to send packs of justiciars off to the Jewish quarters: where they dispense justice, where they read their briefs, where, equipped with no more proof than their own savagery, sometimes brilliant, they accuse the sons of Abraham of pouring the plague into the fonts of holy water by means of little phials. So earnestly did the inventors of the new world wish to import supposedly exotic diseases, in guise of proof, that the less wise among them effectively brought back never-before-seen plagues in their laundry — but God, theirs if he exists & mine own if he holds water, prevents me from adopting a surgeon's precision on this subject: he would sooner spare me those details.

These imaginary diseases, we have undoubtedly called them venereal so that the camouflage might be the more effective, and to muddy the waters whilst stoking our imaginations — if the plague spreads with a baleful ease, without surprise but without peripeteias, as if it were spread on the wind alone and with a fatality verging on boredom, the diseases of love for their part suppose so many exchanges, trades, compromises, sharings, colloquies, congresses, lies, festivities, transfers, efforts, loans, partnerships, glissades, swaps, and amusements that the sick men at least have the consolation of living through an adventure and experiencing their share of that universal love, seemingly the lot of all mankind. This poison now popular like the latest trend, but natural as the course of water down a slope, most often proves fatal; it opportunely replaces those other poisons that were in use not so long ago, shortly before the invention of the new world, when to make an inheritor, political candidate, or military officer disappear, you had to crush up powders in a mortar. Nothing could be more practical than to replace those dubious and not always effective potions (sugar masks the bitterness of digitalis, but vitiates the effects of cyanide) with an epidemic from which no innocents are safe and which hardly conceals the signs of its effects. Only opinionated types of Dr. Fracastoro's ilk were able to recognize the symptoms of a fever well known to doctors, endemic to the area around the swamps of Rome and the back alleys of Naples, thus rejecting the hypothesis of a disease newly contracted from red-skinned slaves, thereafter diffused from bunk to bunk. I have counted this Fracastoro among my friends, ever since the day I had the good fortune to cross paths with the doctors of Padua; on the faith of many, he is a just man, yet the promoters of the new world doggedly deny the evidence, so that their opinions may prevail over those of garrulous doctors. Wisely, they foresaw that it would become fashionable, hardly different from the latest infatuation; in fact, ever since the day they managed to convince the people that Isabella the Catholic herself died of it, the new world pox has been spreading like a refrain.

You do not seriously think that this Catholic, your foremother & the unequivocal ruler of all Europe, of the Empire by anticipation, she by whom this country became a country, she who reinstated the old Inquisition, put the crucifix back in conference rooms, just as she restored Christ to the cross in order to educate her people, you do not seriously imagine this matchless Isabella let herself be seduced by some hidalgo, or let herself be wooed by one of her admirals newly returned from India, that she let him dishonour her, pollute her in that way, thus insulting her virtue and the law of St. Paul. Nor could you imagine, I do not think you could, Ferdinand compromising himself with one of those swarthy, mortified women, scared stiff from so much submission, brought back from Sumatra, disguised in Etruscan costume, moreover polished, but exhibited to the public as sinners or temptresses, demoniacs, part of their natures unveiled without much modesty, since it is said the antipodes know aught of privacy. (These are all but hypotheses of course, the historian's role being to collect them all, without distinctions of style, bugs and lice & all.

Only the prince is in a position to judge the good & the bad, and to say to which shall be accorded the right of survival.)

Nothing is more explicitly false than the hypothesis of a death by the great pox, and nothing more doubtful than its approbation by the public. Soon the day may come when it will be affirmed that Philip the Handsome himself died of syphilis, that Joanna the Mad contracted her madness in the same way — that Enrique IV too, rightly prostrate in the barque of his adulterers, would also have tasted that delicious & pulverulent death, he of whom it is notwithstanding said that he went to Heaven as virgin as a jellyfish, which he more or less was, in a few respects.

At the antipodes, the currents reverse, the winds blow backwards, every living and non-living thing is subject to the retrograde movements of the cosmos, thus of time, it's quite natural. We know from the *Politicus* of Plato that in the southern hemisphere men pass from old age to childhood &, having become children again, are engulfed and vanish; we also know that certain fruits in distant countries rejuvenate those who eat them. You will see me perhaps one day cede to temptation; then will I go and bathe in the fountain of youth or taste such marvellous fruits. Doing so will allow me to get my wisdom teeth back, then my milk teeth, sharper but more fragile, and it will help me to regain enough of my former strength; I will go and I will slap some of these fake doctors, fake sailors, fake suitors, as they descend from the caravels (I will slap the caravel too).

Our churches are emptying out in Leipzig, the heretics have announced that the true nail of Christ conserved at St. Peter's in Rome is a shameful trinket. The cardinal of Cisneros and the Catholic Kings just as soon deemed it necessary to urgently recruit some new adherents, from the supposedly newfound lands, shellfish trawlers who converted more spontaneously & more rapturously than the Jews of Seville under the tender eye of the God of Jacob (but with the help of Vincent Ferrer's aspergillum). Brought naked to the doorsteps of our baptisteries, inspired by that sense of newfound freedom that comes of stepping out of a crowded wagon, they gladly vow allegiance to the religion of Isabella, especially when they are given holy water and see unfurling over their heads the decorations of the temples where we repent our sins. Since they speak none of our languages, a priest mimes the Gospels for them, up to the Passion. That ensures many new members set down on our lists, when north of the Scheldt believers full of excessive fervor are dancing around Luther's placards. Whether the new world exists or no, this matters not a whit, so long as the naves are full up again; so much the worse if the fresh converts be not bankers or jewelers, instead just idle souls found in the desert by a well, like the Samaritan was.

This was the state of things a little before Luther arrived, endowed with the mug of a lean lard vendor and incessantly hollering, *Ich bin nicht, Ich bin nicht.* Luther? a mystic? a minuscule monk borne along by a gust? a troublemaker who would have worn the monk's habit for twenty years to hide his traits as well as his intentions? one of those good plump men whom Europe is partial to in times of crisis, whom leaner men promote to give their plots an appearance of solidity? or the agent of Satan, who realized that he needed to seem a little less unapproachable? What if Luther, disguised as a priest, stuffed full of theology & touched by lightning, were an agent of commerce, an employee of the banks? what if the question of indulgences raised all over Europe right now is but some idle chattering of monks and soteriologists slaying each other in Latin, but dealing out drubs with titmouse plumes? Then Luther would have come into the world not to rock our old boats, but to denounce the percentage that the Fuggers' bank gets on every payment of deniers in exchange for indulgences: not less than fifty percent (that's a fact). Luther, the agent of a rival bank, would have only nailed up his grievances in order to denounce that monopoly — the rest being but agitations of cardinals around a fornicating pope, actions of intellectuals on the prowl for debate, with the foundries and printing presses happier than ever to sell pamphlets & counter-pamphlets by the thousands, texts for and texts against, like so many loaves of Tiberias.

The *mundus novus*, savages to convert, a spotless garden for the Christians? a reserve of captives, rather, hard workers, indefatigable early risers. Perhaps, but then one has to wonder why anyone would go off into the horizon to look for natives found as recently as yesterday just a stone's throw away, by idle sailors accustomed to sailing up and down the coastline (the kind who panic if they lose sight of the coastline), why anyone would claim to be bringing back slaves from the useless islands who were formerly brought over dry land, and sometimes on their own two feet, from Chio via Constantinople? Such were the questions I was asking my parrot yesterday, when the parrot & I, perhaps even the parrot before me, we remembered a royal decree of 1477, probably signed by Enrique the Abulic, his hand slowly guided by that of a bishop, his head propped up by two midgets normally employed as fly-swatters: this decree affirmed that the red half-negrœs of the Canaries were Christians united with us in God's love & in Revelation, and that to this effect a soul had descended into their bodies through the nostrils, as well as the breath of the God of Moses, & that by virtue of this they are exempt from slavery because true Christians are not to be so subjugated, even though their bodies may be covered with scarifications which they now abjure; and by the same token, the Abulic threatened to punish the merchants who were guilty of having locked up baptized negrœs in cages.

Of course, after his decree of prohibition, it took more than a week for the steady stream of recruits and captives to run dry, brought back from Africa in caravels between barrels of fish and others, full of alcohol, sometimes containing a precious elephant's foot, cut with care just below the first joint, prepared for the meals of Sardanapalus and the daughters of Elagabalus. For many months, even years afterward, the inhabitants of the Spanish or African littoral could still see those shackled creatures being transported like so many boughs of dead wood, as indifferent to their fate as to the currents bearing them away to the city centers. At the time of the signing of the ordinances of October 1500, their traffic was taking place under forest cover, since in that setting avarice is blended with the ill intentions and mean machinations of creeping vines and snakes, the traps and pitfalls of a humanity caught betwixt fright and appeals to magic. The weakest natives, those who will belong to the tribe of the conquered for many years to come, who will only have to shake their shackles to sound the lament for liberty lost, will go on being captured, until in the marketplaces of Genoa or the trading posts of Madeira, they are at last deemed superfluous, given away as meager and lamentable bonuses on the sale of some precious wood, sold by the ton. One fine day, the law intervenes, that famous ordinance is published which saved, in the Balearic Islands, the captives of La Gomera among others, requiring their immediate liberation, under threat of prosecution. At roughly the same time, the dark black or ochre inhabitants of the desolate lands saw the bishop Juan de Frías bending over backwards to help them, undoubtedly an heir to Christ's indulgence, if not also to the well-fed indulgence of the last vicars of Rome: in the Canaries, this agent for good allied himself with the Guanches contra the merchants and their merchandise (Moses's speech or, in a more clever vein, that of Paul, contra the culverins) as if playing a part in a newfangled gospel, or illustrating his own gilded legend in advance. Thus, almost overnight, our entrepreneurs found themselves unfairly frustrated by a workforce that had to be assembled on site, workers with the rigidity of steers who have long worn the yoke and who go about their labours with indifferent obduracy, which is at least reliable, and patiently instilled; moreover, they are now required to pay a fair wage to their workers, woodcutters, men from here, to replace their slaves in the pine forests of Leiria.

Along the gunwales of their caravels, and sometimes seated on crates, they wept, in order to arouse their creditors' pity, insensible to the ruin of others as to all forms of sorrow, save when their own finances are at stake. The merchants, after having wept a little for the box seats, then filed suits, lost them, and filed appeals; ermine sleeves and felt hats went head to head over the course of long debates in the tribunals, at the end of which, inevitably, nine times out of ten, the timber merchant of men found himself obliged to release his slaves — but understand, Sire, not simply by returning them to the Ocean, as we reject a shell whose colours we have sufficiently admired, but by returning them to their families. When the annunciation of the new world began to be bruited here and there, in the courts and in the lousy lanes, heralded by cartographers proud of their cartographies and sailors squandering their wages, the ordinances protecting the baptized negrœs from slavery were intended to prevent other captures, effected by the imagination on the far side of the world. But these laws set down on scraps of leftover paper were in vain, at so great a distance; vain too were the remonstrances of the Franciscans and the few pudors of provosts tempted by the ideal of charity, quickly forgot. Were it necessary to find in this skein of ambitions a single explanation for the invention of the new world, it would be this: when ordinances wax constraintive, when bishops prove supercilious, when the entire western coast of Africa is considered as the exclusive fief of the Portuguese missions, then some vulpine men, skilled enough to turn the maps over with a single hand, go off to root out an unseen country situated beyond the last known meridian, beyond the tumultuous seas, where they tell us that diamonds grow in the trees, thinking this lends their fables a semblance of verisimilitude. They devise islands in the form of beans or crescent-moons, they lodge there all the various one-horned beasts contained in our literature, then bring men and women into being, and on perfectly virgin soil, unleash those savages to whom they impute crimes more foul than the still unspeakable crimes of Gomorrah. Barred from subjugating the Guanches, they bring this new race of anthropophagi into existence and fit a ring of iron or leather about the criminals' necks once and for all, very little maintenance required. All Europe, its kings' heads, its bobbing bishops' heads and, even more bobbing still but in a derisory and dancing way, the heads of the poets exalting mankind, all of Europe approves of the hunt on the sole condition that neither Scripture nor pity shall prohibit these carnivorous beings from being deemed beasts of burden, who walk about not only naked, but beyond the reach of our laws. According to the least duped, the new caravels of Spain, after brushing the Portuguese coasts, sail out past the trading posts, exceeding not only Cape Verde, but also the Red Cape, the Yellow Cape, and Cape Bojador where the waters of the sea sometimes boil, then they go hunting after ochre negroes and cast their nets in the Canary Islands once again: but, in order to make their captures legal, they are obliged to generate stories of unknown islands that no one will go verify, especially not magistrates stricken with gout; they invent blood crimes, incests based on what they themselves know of incest, and nefarious repasts. If captivity can pass for punishment, it can be sanctioned anew, in these islands of Cariba, or Caniba, or Caliba (the accounts diverge), and the Catholic Kings, yesterday so scrupulous, or the pope himself if he ventures outside his bedroom, look on the conquerors' pious work with approval, and even employ at very little cost five or six of these red men as broom-pushers. A free zone is declared, on paper, a so-called group of islands, in truth a blurry perimeter in the middle of the sea and fog, where there are none but jellyfish to sing the praises of God and mark the presence of life on earth. Trade starts up again, the captures are sanctioned as legitimate by each and all, the caravels are loaded full again, the merchants abandon the tribunals, as soon as they kneel down their rights are reinstated, and soon they are making bands of ochre negrœs march about at nine thousand maravedís a head, with the pride of St. Michæl when he smote the Serpent. Later, the free zone will be miraculously enlarged (a dash of the plume is all it takes), and the fair will be in full swing when the young monks and officers deprived of their bonuses shout themselves hoarse to decry the crooked dealings.

Because they fear no contradiction and because sometimes the best disguise for the imposture is a spaniel's candor, the authorities have called these fabricated islets "useless islands," buoys loosed in the ocean sea, where the anthropophages go afrisking. According to those who claim to have made the voyage, the smell of barbecue and of acrid stew, of grease and of burnt hair reigns there, and the savages would preserve in brine tubs or between their teeth morsels of flesh that once belonged to our priests, to rosy children who left Seville to breathe the sea air, on the forecastle, holding down their skirts. But, as we know, there is no worse liar than a returning voyager, especially if he is returning from nowhere, if he was content to only cut the wake in circles before watching it die, be weakly reborn, before ultimately dying — there is no worse liar: starting with the lost child of Ithaca who brought back from his fugue stories of Calypso and of war without mercy. On this side of the world, the law prevails, functions, which is to say gives rise to libraries and librarians, grants a legal form to worry and suspicion, complicates protocol, relies on well-reasoned but austere sets of contradictory obligations, joins the motley mess of man to a garrison rigour, invents a strange poetry based in exactness, periphrasis, redundancy & literal meaning, also organizes bullfights in courtroom aisles between men in black and men in velvet robes, who surprise themselves with their ability to go full force without spilling a drop of blood — the Law prevails, the law according to which we all scurry along: thus, to legally complement the enslavement of ochre negrœs supposedly brought back from the useless islands, the judges together with some priests open inquests, organize missions, send on location, which is to say towards the abyss, teams of consuls & orthodox theologians, to determine which tribes are guilty of consuming human flesh and distinguish those tribes from the rest of the Christian world: infamy, my Prince, resides less in slavery than in this distinction exercised by such good men.

Brought from Guinea, the ordinary Blacks used to sell for eight thousand maravedís a head; we are told that the ochre negrœs from the useless islands, hastily painted to give an exotic impression, cost one thousand five hundred to be captured, fed, and disguised; sold then for nine thousand or more, they reap a handsome profit, almost unprecedented. To pull the wool over our eyes no doubt, & draw profit from the Great Invention, Bartolomeo Colombus, brother of Cristóbal, did not shy away from such revenues: for him it was a way to convert the fable into a clanging currency, transform balderdash into revenue, & headless monsters into *doblas castellanas* and *doblas magnas*, coins weighing nearly half a pound each (I speak now from hearsay, you may be skeptical, Sire, my fortune or bad luck never having permitted me to weigh more than three little coins in my old palm, like a chick pea in a grain shovel). Others besides him partook in the dance too, who bent their knees & lifted their legs higher, including that Ovando, master of Alcántara, of whom I have spoken before and who, among all the impostors, is the most comfortable, the most swaddled, most well-nourished and least sympathetic, with a few exceptions: that man knew how to extract from Isabella an authorization to enslave the phantasmatic Caribas of the imaginary Ante Illa. It is said that the father superior had so many hands at his service that he rivaled God among his thousands of angels, and also His beatitude, when a thousand manicured fingers hastened to relieve at an instant's notice, with little fingernails, an itch, on the underside of his groin. Caniba, Caraïbes, Calina, Carila, Caribi or even Galibi: I persist in my belief that all these names which look alike but seem so farflung, having made their way here from the decidedly empty west to designate eaters of men with faces of dogs, were but the various attempts of slave traders to find the right word that would finally satisfy supercilious priests, much as sales merchants pronounce ten fanciful prices before stating the actual, the better to delight the buyer.

Shelves surround me, on which are assembled the *Quattuor Navigationes* published in Germany, the *Cosmographiæ Introductio* issued from the workshops of the Waldseemüllers, the *De Ora Antarctica* printed by Hupfuff, the first *Decades* of Peter Martyr and of course the journal of Columbus (as well as a certain number of his letters to his nurse, penned from prison). I dust these books off even if doing so dazes me, I ensure their peaceful retirement even though they endanger me, for they open a breach into which the salty waters of the open sea go swirling. To contradict them, I will not light a back-fire, I mistrust matches and my modest abode risks not to survive a conflagration; to contradict them, I would have to stock a library of the same width and size with mine own zealous writings, which would furnish curious persons with a curious distraction, if not proofs, too.

My hypotheses, I find myself perfecting them in my solitude, though certain of them, I was able to hear by snatches, in the Chancelleries, spoken in hushed voices: for talk sometimes leaks out of the palaces, where the ears of attentive persons lie open and listening. Under cover of anonymity, some diplomats evoke the fate of the red-skinned slaves (and two or three priests worry themselves over it, whilst rocking back and forth like pendulums), as other gentlemen of Foreign Affairs prefer to evoke the doge, gravely shaking their heads. For, according to these informed men, the invention of the new world is but one tactic among several in the war Portugal and its allies are quietly waging on such cities as Venice, so brazen and so powerful in the Mediterranean: offensives are staged that consist half of folklore, of pageantry, of grandiloquent gests & fortunes — for the other half, of battles fought at sea according to the most classical strategies. Venice the enemy declared long ago, once and for all: because of its small size, because of its bridges constructed over the waters to the Indies, the true Indies, those of the Orient, because of its alliance with the Mamelukes and its traffic in the Red Sea. As early as the time of Afonso V, Portugal was staging offensives up and down the African coasts against the city of Venice & its arrogant monopolies; after sailing past the Cape of Torments, rebaptized the Cape of Good Hope, the merchant sailors were smart enough to obtain great quantities of pepper, which they brought back to all of Southern Europe, soon even reaching Anvers. And it's a curiosity of these modern times, Sire, to see conflicts fought not with gunpowder or old arquebuses, but instead with volleys of pepper, as if by sprinkling spices on the enemy one could finish him off, and have the added pleasure of seeing him admit defeat in a great sneezing fit. That is how wars are fought, by means of little berries —perhaps tomorrow we will see our catapults hurling bananas and our artillery men burning cinnamon at the gates of besieged cities. Thus does Portuguese pepper set Venice all atremble, since it comes here to compete, and because its prices are unbeatable — this milk that suckling children need, a Venetian used to say, it's pepper, absolutely: the virtual lifeblood, so to speak, of that city insane enough to stake its fortune on so insubstantial a thing. Many parties, one after the other, have contributed to the commercial defeats of Venice, cruelly beset by Portugal and by its king, who soon will decide on the official rate of the spice and, conscious of the stakes, knowing that he holds in the palm of his hand a weapon that will bring the doges to their knees, will soon make the pepper trade into a monopoly of the State; in Lisbon and elsewhere guards are watching over spice-stocks just as all over Europe we jealously guard the powder-kegs in the arsenals. At sea, all up and down the coasts of the black continent and in the ports, Portugal prevails, with the ease of a jolly merchant sure of his business and soon dozing atop his many bags of silver; it dominates the markets of the Netherlands and England, both delighted to finally taste less insipid repasts in their permanent fogs. One day five ships will majestically penetrate to Falmouth, swaying, hard to manœuvre as though they were chock-full of the spices, which they are, abrim with pepper and saffron from Calcutta, while in its dereliction, in the whirlpool brought on by its shipwreck, the Venetian fleet — its galleys, piteous galleys

— will be unable to get pepper for a decent price anywhere, not at Alexandria nor in Beirut (empty-handed, they will return to their country & take up the prayers suitable in such times of dearth). Still later, it will be Germany, Ravensburg in particular and the Magna Societas, who will betray Venice by resolving henceforth to eat only pepper from Portugal; then the City will have to employ every ruse it can, seal up its borders, hold on tight to its protectorates, ally itself to Egypt, incite it to attack the holy places of Palestine, ask the sultan to address the pope, somehow arrange for Amir Husayn's galleys to do battle with Portugal's ships, nothing will work.

It is by consequence not too bold a wager to suppose that the purpose of this new world, dryly devised in the palaces of Seville, perhaps with the half-envious, half-amused complicity of its sometimes enemy & circumstantial ally Portugal, is foremost to upset Venice, already half-decayed, to taunt it by situating voluptuous islands out of its reach, seeing how it is stuck between the maw of Italy and that of Istria — isles where pepper is to be had in ever greater quantities, along with cinnamon, coriander seeds, and countless other riches that never make it into the official inventories. The advantage of doing business that way, on paper, moving miniature boats about on a map of the world without ever leaving one's office, is that it costs not a florin, no more than the price of the ink and paper; the colporteurs whose job it is to propagate the invention of the new world in Venice are for the most part mercenaries, happy with three times nothing, and they drink to forget.

The other advantage is that, if by chance Venice remembers the Polo brothers and gets the urge to go drop anchor in the New Indies, its sailors will likely only discover a bit of whalebone & water, only water, neither gold nor cardamom, nor rhubarb, only a great many reefs, far too many for their meager galleys.

As Portugal does with pepper, Spain does with gold, in the hopes of making Venice sink down once and for all into that lagoon in which it belongs (some say). All of the gold on the African coast, of the Sudan, of Ethiopia, of the estuary of Senegal and of Niger, and the jewels of Guinea, of Ceuta and of Tlemcen, all of these disguised as nuggets originating from newfound islands reach Europe and compete with the wealth of the Venetians, whereat they grow worried, and spend long hours recounting their assets in preparation for the coming collapse, embarrassed to the east by the Turks, elsewhere by toing-and-froing galleys and Ragusian pirates. While Spain, thanks to its imposture heralded from town to town, waxes rich and exhibits bulging safes, the Venetians bite their nails and pawn their family jewels: and already here and there people are saying the ducat is not what it used to be, that it disappears from the banks and from pockets only to rejoin, pitifully, the pages of ledgers, where that magnificent money scantily balances the books, satisfies the pinch-pennies and melts into a mathematics of pure addition and subtraction. There is probably some connexion between the pepper berries brought from the shores of Paradise, oriental or occidental, & gold in its flake or powder form, that gold which was elsewhere said to be the very substance of the people (& of which Christopher

Columbus himself affirmed that whosoever possesses it assures his soul's entry into paradise). Doubtless some promoters of the new islands have found amusement in the concordance of pepper and gold, doubtless they willingly hit upon similar motifs, alternating in their way between the derisory and the sublime, it being admitted that gold is sublime and pepper derisory. Gold and pepper as but a single way of waging war on Venice's merchants, hardly different the one from the other: moreover, and still to the same point, it would suffice to recall that pepper, like money, is subject to its falsifications: there exists a fake pepper, called lalaguette, out in convoys and on our plates.

The fake does not have the qualities of the true, it only appears to have them; yet, at the risk of pleading against mine own cause, I must admit that the efforts used by counterfeiters often merit far greater attention (from customs officers, among others) and admiration than their authentic models, which take no further trouble than to simply exist: resting on an embroidered cushion until the end of recorded time. Certain ruses of the falsifiers even earn the applause of an enraptured audience prior to a sentence from a judge in the commercial courts, and the risks incurred, because they require haste in the composition and foster virtuosity, from the tip of the rod. Alas, of late, the defrauders are gradually relinquishing their art, so much so that the qualities dissembling the falsehood start to thin out, to let the tinpot truth shew forth all the more brightly — and, by reconciling their appearance to their essence, the fake jewels no doubt hope to find, in the eyes of their manufacturers, a form of honesty that is all their own. Fake saffron is now no more than fake saffron, fake pepper looks and tastes like fake pepper; amateurs of comparisons lose yet another opportunity to exercise their regard, or even to see halfwits falling into sophisticated traps — sophisticated as metaphors.

The new world is a promise, pronounced here, on our soils, and today; the new world would effectively be a tomorrow we await indefinitely but which in actuality never comes, since only another today arrives, with the dawn, with the morning, with the frosts, with the farmers heading to market, dry bread and black olives, as always under the same veiled skies. Ultimately this new world, under that aspect of an ever-promised, never-honoured tomorrow, is a speculation, first opened by the non-dupes, but insincerely, then pursued by the dupes, but tenaciously. The conquerors in suits of iron and bronze, gladly gleaming and cruel, sounding like so much sheet metal, textile merchants, goldwashers and lapidaries incapable of concealing their jubilation at the time of departure, linked to the gold market, titillated by the idea of going where even Ulysses himself did not go, there where monsters skip in circles about paradisiacal palm-trees — all of these men quit our shores, they embark, they charter sardine boats to conquer the new islands, but before leaving spend months convincing other dupes, other cozeners, as susceptible to the sound of the word maravedís as others to the word Scheherazade. They depart only after having borrowed astronomical sums from the usurers, whom they promise to pay back tenfold, with that boldness characteristic of those who have nothing left to lose. But these merchants, gold-washers & conquistadors, whether gleaming or rusty, do not only leave with loans from banks and small-time lenders, they leave the country also with loans from each and every one of us, with miserable pledges (two or three negroes from the Canaries disguised as natives, two or three nuggets from San Jorge de la Mina, two or three costumes from the Dalmatian coast): we lend them an incredible amount for these curios, at a great loss surely, for we loan our confidence, our hopes, our judgements and our capacity to resist and contest the fables, the figures, the misleading geometries; in addition to the monies they extract from us or the loose change of the Fuggers, they also take our approbation, our faith, on the promise of dividends that are the new world itself, in its entirety, & so many fine tomorrows. Of cheated lenders, we are the most ruined, especially when we would prefer not to admit our bankruptcy: so long as the calendar convinces us of the existence of tomorrow, instead of complaining, the lenders tally up their interests.

The new world is a promise of reimbursement, it is in its entirety the reimbursement long past due to the bankers and naive dupes of this old world, in other words it is the total interest on the debt (that would be its exact definition); yet just as true reimbursements are always slow in the coming, the debt meanwhile grows and the debtors, for once richer than their creditors, pay for their tardiness with more promises. Some of us potato-eaters are weak enough to believe the promises piling up on top of each other, but sooner or later, me or my neighbour, we have had it, finally grown wise to the extent of the arrears. Everyone, whether a lender or a borrower (when not a matter of gold but of fine words, usury enriches the debtor) has no choice but to add thereunto; the eternity that the speculators and sham governors of the New Indies grant themselves by choice or by necessity is this perpetually postponed tomorrow that would not be Judgement Day, but rather the Day of Settling All Debts: here we are, condemned to believe in the future, not for its sake, but to convert our poverty into a very long-term loan. The new world? like the horizon it recedes at our approach, like the interest on a debt it grows fatter from month to month, but it can quite easily never come to pass, simply existing in written form, in account books of a disarming abstraction (no one is required to keep their promises, they only have to be forever about to: there is a tension that keeps us alive, by force).

My prince, be wary also of those who adopt, toward your empire and its protectorates, the stance of gold-diggers: the crouched, broke-back posture of zealous men who squat down to pulverize through a sieve the soil over which you would apply your authority. That is a vulgar atomism, confirmed by facts, by the derisory fragmentation of dirt or of an entire mountain sifted through the crossed fingers of a greedy man; 'tis an avarice ever on the lookout for dross & so long encrusted with mud as to be therefrom inseparable, an avarice that walks hand in hand with a philosopher's derision, a philosopher in clogs and in shackles, for whom impermanence is not just a play on words or the perception of the flight of time, but the very principle of his work — a secret of his métier. To win little, to know the proportion of gold and of miry water, to divine profit potentials by referring to the price at which gold is indexed, to ambition to force the whole world through a riddle in order to stuff up a hole in a tooth, the gold washers, your gold washers, your avant-garde in the newly colonised lands, cultivate a smooth cynicism free from feeling and from cabotinage, which is no lucid demonstration in the style of Diogenes, but a way of life.

SIX
What Follows, et cetera

The invention of the new world and of the useless islands supposed the invention of evidence, fabricated on this side of the earth, on the continent, in the Portuguese colonies perhaps, but always brought back in to port; for it is impossible to make a country of fog, of phantoms and of gleaming gold exist out there without having some exotic but tangible scraps wash up on our beaches. Some talk might have sufficed: our taverns are full of those boasters returned from afar, full of one-armed men who clasped in an embrace the Great Khan of China and the incestuous gang of Prester John, full of blind men who saw Gihon and Pison, full of myopics who caught a glimpse of the Queen of Sheba's jewels and have never been the same since. Talk was an abundant staple but, for the benefit of the jeering peasants who recognized old fables from Pliny and Amadis in the official reports, it was thought wise to present more solid evidence, even if only sacks stuffed full of pebbles. Ultimately, the campaign was so well effected that everything which happens seems as if by magic to confirm the invention and proclaim on its behalf, even the humblest of facts and most shameful of misadventures, including peripeteia usually occurring only in the privacy of four-poster beds, and what, in years past, would have more than sufficed to refute the imposture. Henceforth, nothing that takes place here retains its autonomy; we must resign ourselves to being in the future nothing more than consequences, the causes of which are to be found amidst the useless islands; this is true of gold, which comes back to us with interest; it is true of the new generations of black and ochre slaves; it is true of that disease of which Queen Isabella is said to have died; it is true also of the illegitimate sons who will come back to us looking like cozened fools.

A few voices advance the idea: these new lands would have been, up until very recently, lands the cosmographers of old sought to shield from the reach of human adventure, perhaps because there was wisdom, a worm-eaten wisdom but wisdom, in silently fixing a limit to the adventures to be had — and even, preemptively, to the failures. All those ship's captains, whose motto is *where everyone else is going thither do I go*, they did not want to heed that silence; to the point that they transformed our ports, our harbours, the inns where the sailors drink their fill, but also the palaces where the speculators speculate, into rendezvous of men on the go (sacred antechambers where all these passions cross paths, size each other up, and assume diplomatic roles, since they speak of what is faraway, all the while dissembling, never to open their valises), without suspecting that in acting so, in their perennial eagerness to go, they are obeying like the lowliest of pages carrying out the injunction of a majordomo. Our alchemists, now lost at sea and diluted therein, used to amuse themselves by interleaving successes and failures in their books:

but it was the failures that gave rise to vocations. The conquerors err when they make the new world out to be the land of success, they err when they ask the poets for hymns of victory, & they err when they ostentatiously announce the proofs of their effectiveness: their overcompetence in these matters will likely culminate in rendering them morose.

As I will presently invite you to, you will begin by distinguishing land alchemy, or dry alchemy, from the alchemy of voyages, or wet alchemy: that is to say, the kind unfolding in the laboratories, in proximity to furnaces and books, under the authority of the masters, from the kind that spreads out over oceans because it thought it saw in certain pages of certain books an invitation to the voyage (and because it confuses the phases of the work with the new islands, the blacksmith's efforts with the adventures of sailors, gold as a pure idea or subject of meditation with gold as the principle of cupidity, primary matter). I explained how this misconception arises, and said that overzealous disciples who would not deign to their labours preferred to go off and hunt for gold at sea instead of fabricating it, exhausting themselves, consecrating their old age to it, and withdrawing from the outside world because alchemy supposes hermetic caves & nocturnal existences. Dry land alchemy is measured, prudent, it is a history of failures (we will soon see how & why), accordingly it counterbalances its satanic vainglory, its pretensions to usurp God in little crucibles, with a de facto humility, which conceals no defeat, but to the contrary elaborates a mythology and a vocabulary of failure, a whole grammar of defeat, so to speak.

Wet alchemy, seafaring alchemy, is the unwitting successor of that science of failure, but it forges ahead, with its youth and its promise to reimburse a thousand creditors, suffers failure in the end, never recovers, learns no lesson from it and knows not how to convert nullity into results. Since this seafaring alchemy, fake alchemy and real cupidity, does not exist apart from the principle of its success, which relies on enthusiasm, it slides right by failure much as a parched vagabond forgoes a stop at the fountain; it only knows (like monarchs) yes as the response to its orders and desires, and adopts an admiral's intransigence on the subject. Dry land alchemy by tradition, as much as by its taste for the *coincidentia oppositorum*, knows to paint failures as successes, thus enlists a complex, interminable, savant & somber rhetoric on their behalf, in order to sublimate them, to dance with them as with the dead, to draw from them yet another work. Seafaring alchemy prefers to ignore insuccess, or rather it swiftly discounts it; either it plays mum, the merchants also keeping silent, with respect to its still empty coffers, or it abolishes everything alike, just as criminals sacrifice accomplices to preclude betrayal.

Dry land alchemy had the wisdom to hush its secrets; that is in truth why failure seems to attend it so frequently, and why it does not consider failure a cause for despair, nor as a refutation or proof of the vanity of its goals, the proof of its errors accumulated over centuries on shelves. How naive to think that the dry land alchemists never had any other goal than to fabricate gold, to multiply it a hundred-fold, and to cover the Earth with that substance so that it flowed out of their furnaces in streams; it's quite the opposite in fact: once the disciples of Hermes figured out how to create gold in their furnaces, they suppressed that hitherto accessible science, and preferred to bemist it in other phantasmagorias, which became the essence of their books. As soon as one looks closely enough at it, alchemy is revealed as the science permitting gold's rarity to be conserved as long as possible, a rarity fragile as the transparency of water — all the work of these anxious, deceitful men, in their laboratories or in their books in various languages, is to hush the secret of gold, the better by drowning it in other hypotheses, by devising recipes whose merit is to distract the undisciplined disciple, multiply the digressions, and so doom the amateurs to salt, to mercury, to the spittle of toads, to oils taken from a young virgin under a crimson moon, to sulfur and alkali, just as one sends an importuner off to the devil.

Among the alchemists, Sire, we also find those two categories of dupers and dupes that the invention of the new world suscitates all across Europe — such that it almost seems to be a question of a more subtle and pacific complicity, excluding foul dealings, when the dupers trick the dupes for their common benefit, until they at last understand. The goldmakers squander their energy and waste their time dissecting texts until they realize, one morning, that all the literature of Hermes is a detour leading them far from gold, and the whole alchemical quest a way to never come into contact with it; then they wise up and hand down their grimoires to younger disciples to lead them astray: thus such existences perpetuate themselves. At the heart of these fabulous books, of this smoke, of these bats, of these fleeced men, there is one singular truth, which is like the pit of an apricot or the diamond said to be hidden at the center of the earth: the law by which rarity confers value, and by which a fabricator of gold with all his wishes granted would reap his own ruin with each new pound of gold he produces in his casseroles. To create lead from lead and watch bankers, naifs, misers, dreamers, poets, children, jewelers *&* masters of usury dance around that tautology — that right there is the sole great work of alchemy. Retention or impotence is the esoteric teaching of Hermes Trismegistus, also known as the Great Empty-Handed One.

It is precisely this wisdom of rarity that the seafaring alchemists ignore, for want of tradition, want of patience: if they fail on occasion, they succeed far too often, and they lack the wisdom to curb their successes; they finish by drowning in gold powder, till they are one and all flayed by it, since they have so much it piles up over their heads.

In fact, the arrival of shiploads of gold is not only an episode in the war quietly being waged against Venice, the invention of the *mundus novus* does not have these battles for its sole motif; the reasons for it are both more numerous and as diffuse as are our notions of the devil: multiple motives united by a single will, still difficult to define, called now by a sort of shorthand "the spirit of the new times." The metal unloaded time and time again (as we have shewn this to be the work of seafaring alchemy, in other words, of a counter-alchemy in love with abundance), the metal spreads across Europe to provoke in short order the ruin of each and all, starting with the usurers, first cuffed because first to rejoice. Ruin and bankruptcy of each and all: if it were permitted to me in my solitude to counterfeit the best prophets of the Old Testament, I would threaten our countries with successive bankruptcies, the first giving rise to others, and with a quiet impoverishment that from this moment on makes our last remaining luxuries into the cheapest scruff. Today when a pound of sheep's meat is priced the same as an entire sheep, I prophecy not horned beasts and winged horses, but palaces emptied of their interiors, gold statues converted into plaster statues, creditors reimbursed with the currency of chimps and beans, or other perishable staples. I am not in a position to wax apocalyptic & alarm the bankers, promise them that soon there will be wind, straw, scarecrows, empty jugs; but today and going forward I see money being burnt like tinder, & coins losing their value; I admit that the lira of Venice, like that of Genoa, is no longer worth what it once was, nor the carlin nor the maravedí of Spain, as if the epidemic, refusing to distinguish between dupes and dupers, were attacking those who first introduced it onto our soil. All and sundry, to the merchants' great amazement, to the shared stupor of the lenders and the bank clerks, each adopting the abnegation of Job or the anger of Esau, each made to be as impotent accessories to the miracle of the transformation of wine into water. Once again, certain dupers found themselves duped, ushering in these new times where the hierarchy of fraudulent activities comes to be reversed; since those who possessed the greatest number of coins were the first impoverished.

I was not of their number, I have not been one of those bankers, at the roll of a dice suddenly rich or poor, at the roll of a dice suddenly saved or damned, as contemptible as a prosperous crook but also a victim of his odd, cruel fate; nor am I an usurious private lender, not even with small sums, as I have never entrusted three sous to a feeble-minded dreamer, so that he might go off and lose them over the horizon, before losing his very own self. But I have been a victim like so many others of these privations, and like them I have seen gold pieces in my drawers transform themselves into rampant, black insects, which I call *tenebrions*, and which nourish themselves on paper. Insofar as my maravedís, my few cruzados, ducats, threatened to have no more value than false tokens, without desiring to I inherited a counterfeit currency, corruptly minted in smoke-filled back rooms. Through bad luck, moneys of an inferior grade always end up in my pockets, always, and refuse to go any further, which just goes to shew to what extent I am able to see myself as the ultimate terminus of these exchange markets governing the circulation of coins: something akin to a cul-de-sac or the last man before the desert, to whom it all comes down, exhausted, on whom nothing is lost. From Europe and its trading posts spread all over the African continent, these false currencies have converged in my rosewood safe, which serves me as my bank; sometimes, at the morning sunrise or evening sunset, when the idea of the new world comes to be associated with the languor of my melancholy, to escape my boredom, to rhyme my rancour to my silence, I rub these small coins made of lead, iron, or bronze alloys; I knead them a little as one does to appreciate the fineness of flour, and, when the gelt goes back into its box, I feel I have shucked the best of what the new world has to offer, or the very essence of what lies in store for us, like the preciously harvested salt-flower. Moreover, I find it so difficult to pay my debts, and settle my accounts with that funny money, that I have recourse to the methods of the poor: oft have I done a moonlight flit, absconding from my unpaid bills, as far away as possible. The new world tempted me then, I must confess it really did; of mine own volition I would have boarded the next boat to put a final end to my outstanding accounts, not to make a fortune, but to put some distance between my natural self and my debt-laden self, if such a thing were possible. (Ultimately, if all of Europe's counterfeit moneys end up in my pockets, Europe is thereby purged of them, & my bankruptcy is pious work.)

Subjugated are those who embark, subjugated are those who stay behind: but which are the more profoundly so? Those who remain on the quay singing the *suave mari magno* could in fact sink faster than those whose drowning is foretold in advance (all it takes is a single glance at the gondolas on which they let themselves embark); those who remain will find it of little use to play the part of saved ones, tallying up their years as old men in the Bible do and pretending to be the most venerable, they in turn will drown too, but in a much slower way, like a man cruelly thrown a life preserver so that his drowning lasts several days. Cheated are those who opened their savings accounts, mortgaged their homes, their daughters, their wives & their tribes, before appraising the remainder of their estate one evening as confidently as though they were setting fire to it; cheated in proportion to the percentage promised by the debtors, or worse, in proportion to the percentage the creditor obtains after haggling, victor and vanquished at once, because he sets the rate at which he will finally be rolled in the dust. To recoup their investment, to be reimbursed? they would have to go off and find the crooks and their small coins in the realm of the dead, because that is exactly where those businessmen have disappeared to: they became shadows in the land of Hades, where all moneys are worthless, excepting what pleasure a game of heads-or-tails might proffer, in the hope that a stroke of luck might bring some small surcease of agony.

I have proof that the world over there is neither a paradise where flesh cedes to fruit and fruit cedes to flesh, nor some peasant country, nor the Garden of Allah, nor a promise of gain, but only the abode of the dead, the shoreless place without bottom where naifs are sent to their perdition. These tall tales await the unlikely imprimatur of the pope, perhaps of the Medicis also, while the truth continues to circulate in a disguised form: then tales of misery, wanderings, and ghosts are told, interrupting colourful stories of conquests like the adventures of Fierabras. Some, without seeming to refute the new world, allege to have encountered choirs of mute men there, of noble allure, stoic to the point of fright, luxuriously apparelled, coifed in velvet toques with swords at their sides after the fashion of itinerant hidalgos: but at the greeting of the voyager, who politely removes his hat, these silent and funereal men respond by doffing not only their hats, but their heads. If the newly invented islands exist, if one could go ashore and dock a rowboat there, they would be effectively this: the abode of the dead, a strand on which our spectres disport themselves: our spectres, which is to say our own selves in a nearby future, dressed in velvet and silk, busy miming the gestures of the old, bygone nobility, with the insistence of men deceased, and that pleasure of repetition respective of creatures henceforth immortal, with finally that macabre extravagance which consoles us of nothing but incites us to act the parts of ridiculous clowns.

The new world as the voyage of Orpheus? as a round trip to the realm of the dead and back, to seek out, instead of one's lost youth, instead of one's erstwhile hopes now keeping company with the disabused demons of the rock bottom, a young girl, so ardently loved that you lose your head over her? We know there are spectres of vanished hidalgos down there, who reappear before the foolhardy to inform them that, a few leagues farther on, there is nothing, save an extinguished light, the end of time & space and, between the deeper & deeper waves, the realm of the dead.

Then, yes, maybe it is worthwhile to let ourselves be lulled by illusions one more time, to pretend to play the game and believe the skimble-skamble (that would be an illusion within an illusion); maybe it is worth it to go there, worth drowning even, if I can be certain at death's door of finding the friends I lost long ago — returning empty-handed, I will mask my defeat, like the others, in tales of conquest, parrots, & rainbow-coloured girls.

SEVEN
Epilogue in Counterpoint

I also must add the following: I accept the hypothesis of a beyond if it means I will find Lorenzo Valla there, that master I so dreamed of having, so that I might ask him how to compose a sound *Refutation*, how render my book solid enough to serve as a wedge, to stop the ships in the harbours of Spain and other nations from scooting off, helped by the tide.

I never did meet my master Lorenzo Valla, I did not rub elbows with him in the silence of the universities or the libraries or in the slightly seditious dark recesses of the laboratories; for me he is simply one of those dead men with whom I converse, in my habit, at my reading table, resuscitated by me with every opened book, much as certain monks revive their patron saints whilst reciting their prayers. He remains that rigorous young man contesting the spirit of his age and such elegantly woven impostures; he remains captain of the schooner or general of the army, he alone, for in a single stroke he upended the Roman Empire and the authority of the popes.

My master had the merit to refute the *Decretals*, he knew how to exhume, by giving the profaners their due, a few anonymous monks, clerks *sans histoire*, forgotten for centuries and glad to be so, he demonstrated that they were forgers responsible for the pact laying out in black and white the pope's authority over his vast dominion. And maybe, after having wrested away from the popes a significant part of their territories, while overriding the authority of the saints, of Sylvester I, of Constantine, and of routine, which cements acts of the will like a waterfall smoothly polishing stone, perhaps after all of that he felt himself strong enough to refute God and his existence, by toppling the arguments of Anselm of Canterbury.

My master Valla took it upon himself to refute a dead pope, a long dead emperor, a legion of theologians enamored of their patrimony and the core of the military orders, interested in questions of property and power; but in the end he attacked only a centuries-old story, handed down by word of mouth, as bewitching as stories of all-night parties that confound day with night, right and left; he refuted in the end a simple document, a counterfeit devised at a passing glance, and vulnerable. I have, for my part, wretched disciple, not a duty to confute a short document, but to send back to nothingness an entire land, and soon to contend with a tide of writing that stands tall before me, a library thirty cubits high, tall as the walls of Camelot or of celestial Jerusalem. I have to deal with not just a *Donation* on parchment, which simpers and mocks the exegetes in an overblown style modelled on an older one, but an entire series of *rarissimes* letters, travelogues, ship's logs, account books, sailor's tales, drunkard's songs, official reports, missions addressed to the popes, maps of the world; not counting bits of exotic wood, fruits brought back from the antipodes, admirable flowers and vistas of vast prairies in the suburbs of paradise, the chants of which can be heard faintly in a waterfall, when the gates remain out of sight; and natives shackled to one another, groups of ochre virgins forcibly stripped nude in order to reveal on what wood our prudery is kindled on the far side of the Ocean. I must refute not only kings, their advisors, diplomats and ambassadors conquered by processions of coffers and parrots, merchants coming and going, soldiers and generals tickled whenever an occasion arises to unsheathe their rusty rapiers — but also the dupes themselves, peasants lingering on the quays, villagers forever excluded from the world of flourishing and prospering trades, paupers perennially excluded from the great discoveries, wretches made to admire the adventures and treasures from afar, whose sole knowledge of the prestigious voyages is the flotsam towed back to shore.

The most difficult, Sire, is not to gainsay the beguilers, who grow rich from the voyages and perpetuate the lie, the most difficult is rather to gainsay the dupes, who stand to lose a lot from the invention but would have still more to lose from my *Refutation*: their self-regard, for example. That new world, they cleave to it because it seems that humans naturally cleave to their last truth, even if arbitrary, as a dying animal to its last expiring breath. They are difficult to convince, and the toughest dupes to crack are those who lost a son to the ocean, probably six furlongs from the nearest port: in the depths of their misery of soot and scree, they defend the lies and bite every hand which draws near. I have seen courtiers and faux admirals, decorated from head to toe; I have confronted ship's captains, Franciscans who came back from the new world in sandals, and who are gleaming today in palaces; I have visited with missionaries, commercial agents, ministers, envoys of the pope, representatives from Ferrara and Siena, negotiators surrounded by the noblest material. All of them lied in more or less the same way, allowing for some differences, all took special care to distance themselves sufficiently from their lie with either sarcasm or commentaries so to be able to cast it off without any seeming contradiction in case the situation sours. In the kitchen-boys and the dupes, the roustabouts who hang around the laundries and wineries, the clerks and professors, the church-goers, I saw only unflagging allegiance, faithfulness to outlast death; and, when they speak of the new world, more often than not they give it (as do I, when I catch myself believing in it) all their affection, all their passion, that sense of sacrifice which makes the best soldiers.

It is not always an exultant task to collect proofs and point out contradictions. Where it fell to Lorenzo Valla, my master without magistrature, to face up to the Church's territories, like a battering ram attacking a city by one of its gates, I for my part consider it my duty to confront the people of dupes, my brethren, to whom I am so firmly bound that their dupery is mine own, as their flesh is my flesh. With difficulty I console myself with the idea that my *Refutation* is not strictly speaking a work of debunking, and uniquely that, but rather an invitation from one dupe to other dupes to listen to how the stories go round and repeat, to see how a counterfeit money circulates, and how the fables of Lucius Annaeus Seneca return to us in an official form, via the Chancelleries.

When faced with a lie, every man thinks it his duty to pronounce the truth, and believes that he just as soon dissolves it, just as Christ with a single word drove off the demon, composed of sarcasm and of sulphur; when faced with liars, every man yearns to crack open the safes of the secretaries and sift through the documents, because he eagerly awaits the triumph, tardy perhaps but nonetheless effective, of experts and jurists over boasters and sham sailors, bona fide bastards and speculators. That would be akin to fighting falsehood with truth: but truth has the disadvantage of being prudent, circumspect, and of keeping quiet as silence is its least impure form, it has the unfortunate habit of introducing itself by way of a question and expressing itself in the conditional; that truth which is made up of timorous silence, of time, questioning, and adumbration fails when it comes face-to-face with the lie, the lie being sprightly, performative, incontestable as a blemish, and possessing the authority of a tocsin or call to prayer. (Truth is sometimes puritan, when spoken by chest-thumping clerks, crazy-for-Christ types who gnaw themselves down to the bone and stick out their heads to be chopped off — 'tis a virtue of men who pronounce themselves perfect, and it resembles a catechism for children, compared to florid, thundering lies, glad to be alive and go astray like bibblers in a tavern.) When faced with a lie, other minds artful but bereft of scruples, owing to their dearth, propose the lie itself, brought from elsewhere and fashioned to new ends; they count on the sword-fighters to kill off the sword-fighters, & the lawyers to debate the lawyers: it is certainly not stupid to ask an usurper to chase off another usurper, but the risk of setting in motion a perpetual swerve is great. When confronted with a lie, finally, certain men, possessed of the skill of the burglar, the acrobat, and the chemist, propose recourse to artifice, because in its purview and according to its language, by the rules of its grammar, the difference between the true and the false loses all meaning, just as in the final circle of Hell the difference between men and women becomes null and void. I remain convinced that the fully consenting credulity of a fable's auditors is akin to cleverness, an exercise of reason, sooner stratagem than naiveté, and that this credulity sharpened at the hearing of fables is the skeptics' greatest strength.

According to Christopher Columbus, that ostler to the imposture, our planet would not be perfectly spherical, but oblong, like the breast of a woman: I do not know what opinion cartographers have of such an affirmation; I wonder what Columbus could have known of the breasts of women; I know only that, if there exists a single place in the world where that claim is true, I promise to build my final resting place there.

Do not see me as a Messiah or an orator, do not see me as preaching truth against falsehood by the burning stake, I will not be among those heretics who rely on the proximity of the flames to restore their bad faith, to evince excellence in destruction, to prove madness in dying whilst eyeing the priests who remain in the ranks, orthodox & wise, convinced by the justice of divine ordeal, by the efficacy of living in fear of hell. Essentially, by disabusing my brethren of their delusions, I risk looking like one of the first or last apostles, whose job it was to render amiable a defeated God rotting upon the cross: would that mine own shortcomings and defeats deliver me from that comparison.

I have known in this world of madmen only one truly sensible person — I infinitely regret, Sire, having to recite for you the banal panegyric of the fool wiser than the wise men or the madman who left his doctors mad; I also regret having to borrow the expedient style of Sir Didier Erasmus, whose good sense starts sooner or later to resemble a neck warmer. Nevertheless, it would appear that the last person to staunchly refuse the illusion of the new world is that Joanna, known as the Mad, whose melancholy keeps her cloistered at Tordesillas; her misdoing would be to munch biscuits, to find time long, life difficult, and the consciousness of living similar to the tortures reserved for Bartholomew; she laments her life devoid of love and bitterly endures old age: that is doubtless enough to constitute a total madness, just as in other circumstances a bit of cuirass and a copper cooking pot were enough to whip together a suit of armour (I am thinking of the unfortunate Alonso de Monroy who during the civil war and before his exile, according to legend, armed himself with whatever he could find).

You know this as well as me: Tordesillas is the place where non-dupes finish out their days, in convents or asylums, where their voices strike the walls, return to the ears of the criers, resound in the interiors of cloisters never escaping save in the form of idiotic stammerings or litanies devoid of sense which the melancholics begin, resume, and reel off to exhaust the patience of men of sounder mind. Should you feel inclined, from duty, to overturn that map of the world and push the *mundus novus* down into the Ocean, then do so with sufficient force, and refuse this time all the money of the Fuggers; your choice must surpass a body of opinions pooled from over half the globe. If you find yourself only skeptical, still doubting whether you are able to muster the authority of a man to whom Europe belongs in its near entirety, you will end up, I prophesy to you, like Joanna, respectfully, faithfully, in accordance with official protocol assigned to a madhouse, with a pendulum swinging to and fro over your head.

In his *De Singularum corporis partium*, Alexander of Tralles evokes the melancholics: in particular certain ones recognizable by their ever-clenched fists, who believe they hold the world in their palm, persuaded it else might go flying off; those idiots at least look out for us and shew some concern for our collective fate, which rests entirely in either of their two hands. A few stubborn individuals, two or three, likewise keep the secret of the new world all to themselves, the secret of its non-existence: that conviction, they too hold it like an olive pit in a tightly-clasped fist.

My courage almost failed me when I was beginning this book, which is a letter, when I surprised myself by confounding dupers and dupes, when I had the conviction that one and the other, in effect, are in the end one and the same, akin to two strangers brought together by an unseen but divined familiarity, coming together to embrace or support one another.

I felt despair when I saw duper and dupe, indistinct from each other, recognize themselves as Siamese twins, to the point almost of reversing roles, and all the while rueing the grounds of their resemblance, like a shipwrecked man, it seems to me, both loves and loathes the raft on which he comes to be refuged. In the beginning, I could sometimes see a duped man become a duper, just as a courtier may rise in favor or a shepherdess become a favourite of the prince (such stories do get told); and I also had the opportunity to see a duper become a dupe, in the moment he realizes that other inventors stand over him — there were thus a great many chassés-croisés, & princes like yourself took to consorting more and more with haggard men still unsure of the roles they were carving out for themselves and others: thus began a confusion, which goes on to this day. (The new world dupery is a collective dupery, but due to certain developments, and for simple and practical reasons, the proportion of accomplices among the dupes is ever on the rise. Of course, to be truly thorough would require exploring how complicity turns out to be a still more profound form of dupery, yet even if complicity is disenchantment itself, there comes a moment when the world's last remaining free dupe holds unto himself the conditions necessary to the survival of the imposture: and paradoxically his power is then immense if the collective delusion is to depend on his credulity.)

Certain of the dupes are disabused by strangers, but usually their disillusionment does not make of them enlightened men, rather freed slaves, proud to slum it with the gang and clink glasses with yet others; other dupes disabuse themselves, in which case the disillusionment is a pain or an accident similar to the shock of pebble against a bamboo rod such as the one that initiated Sian-ien to the secrets of his religion. Far more often those ones mope and fret, either resuming their silence which is the least bad way of being alone, or they recriminate in broken phrases, so to further gouge the wound, or instead take to preaching by the roadside, and entertain themselves by swapping the name of Saul for that of Paul, or they are counted as fools for having read too many books, or they become prophets, which means being all of that at the same time. More rarely, though not unheard of, the dupes who disabuse themselves become accomplices to the fraud, the most frenetic if they view their disillusionment as a proof of purity or a mark of merit, the most discreet if they adhere with the sole aim of soothing their pain; their attitude depends on that insidious portion of doubt present at the heart of lucidity, on their suffering, and the remedy best suited to its relief: fisticuffs, mysticism, or farce.

In many instances the accomplices renounce their lies from lassitude: I know of one Diego Álvarez Chanca, a physician to the Catholic Kings and recognized member of the alleged expeditions to the west. He went away, it is said, with pocketfuls of freshly minted money, and his heart swelling with the passion of mercenaries who have been cajoled by their own selves rather than by their masters; but he was soon seen returning, alone or nearly so, despondent, tearing his hat, emptying out his pockets on the quay to pay his return trip, definitively ruined and, according to the most reliable of witnesses, in the throes of the malady he had so often contained up until then, in his patients, with the use of tourniquets for example. Later in life, Diego Chanca never did denounce the inventions, vociferation was not in his practitioner's nature, and moreover the hemmed-in space of a library is hardly suited to publicity; he could no doubt have written this *Refutation*, and addressed it to you while profiting from such authority as wounds confer. Instead, being more canny and more sinuous, Diego preferred to compose in Seville, where he knew a barnacle's death, his *Tractatus de Fascinatione*, a 400-page *in-folio* dedicated to the maladies of vision and the illusions to which they give rise. If one were to raise up to God a library of imposture, this book would have its place between the letters of Peter Martyr and Marco Polo's *Description of the World*, as written by Rusticiano da Pisa.

Hence, I fear at times that I too will end up like those dupes of the new world: believing, fooled, escorted by tales, ready to leave on a raft to drown myself in the open sea, there where the world ends, where it runs off into absurdity; I fear that I will find my defeat more reposeful than a never sure victory, ever demolished, rebuilt, lain to waste, built up again, and ultimately exhausted. I have however assembled around me shelves of books: they declaim in my favor, even if they belong to that race of antique monsters which are regarded today with only charity, the opposite of fright, at best with the interest of an amateur of curiosities, a savant drawn to the leather of the stillborn calf; I know I might find so much stupefying intelligence in their pages; I do not seek, though, to join the ranks of those who make of their own unraveling such a sublime sport.

This present written refutation, addressed to you as neither a rebuke nor a prayer, I refuse to compare it to those messages of distress stuffed into amphoras and entrusted to the immensity of the Ocean, which find their posterity on the sea floor, or to compare it to those calls for help which shipwrecked men, with the ink of the octopus, pen on pieces of tree-bark. If I were to entrust my text to the waters, whether out of melancholy or from a perverse predilection for risk, or if I were unable to do otherwise, or because a great tempest were imminent (but nevertheless with that exacerbated care of certain lapidaries, as they build a fortress about a single pebble), if by a stroke of wisdom I were to equate the immortality of my text with its disappearance, the latter guaranteeing the former, I would do as Christopher Columbus did. It is said that the admiral enveloped the story of his discovery in cerecloth, sealed it in a block of wax, and placed the lot in a barrel which he cast into the sea, after tying it with a very long rope to the prow of his ship: in case of shipwreck, boat and men and riches sinking to the bottom, the tale would continue to dance up at the surface, for any of the curious, the passersby, lost there.

Lost curious ones, in any case grammarians: I fear, like so many little demons in the absence of the one true devil, commentators and analysts coming from the Lateran or those chiming in from Córdoba, creatures rich with a theoretical impedimenta resembling an embalmer's kit. I dread a balm of commentary about the cadaver of my book, especially if the commentary is astute, if it be unanswerable, never faltering, if it advances like a blade; I shun all those who understand and then explain, and thus seem to distribute a manna originating from deep within themselves; I dread their air of generous saints and benefactors, in the halls of Alcalá, in love with a humanity they keep on their knees; I dread them and I distrust them not as the devil but as a charlatan convinced that he is the devil because he fills his absence so overzealously, that was foreseeable; I dread these beings living in the harmony of review and synthesis, because in their profound understanding there resides a profoundly carceral instinct; I exorcize equanimity, as the harmony of success; I relegate to the antipodes of my empire, if I have one, those creatures who have renounced every last worry; I curse those on whom nothing is lost and who, once they have turned a book's last page, are convinced they have done all that there was to do, & rejoice in that tautology, as they might at the fulfillment of a duty.

Here I am like so many, torn between the feeling of having been tricked and the knowledge of having to do battle with curtains stirred by the wind, at the risk of finishing head first in a cape that gives way; I am fighting phantoms, perhaps, and no battle is more arduous than the one that leads the fencer to plant his sword in vain betwixt the ribs of a skeleton. At times it seems as though the shadows at which I thrust are provoked only by my candle, set beside the hand that writes, and by gestures of which I am no longer fully conscious. To declare the truth starts me falling in the void, expressing it perfects my solitude and drives my nearest neighbour still farther away (I have very little use, undoubtedly, for a near neighbour); I surprise myself sometimes by giving the liars credit, and approving the idea of a new world, its naked and suffering natives, its gold pits and its acres, so that I might at last have some solid enemies to pummel, not just draughts of air and phantasms of Lucretius as little real as the memory of a dead woman, yet as troubling.

My hard head notwithstanding, I find myself admitting a few fables from time to time, in order to taste the lies being offered to my brethren and also because I share certain weaknesses in common with them, including that of yielding to temptation on the pretext of sharpening my abstinence and, lastly, because by withdrawing from the polemic for an instant I find a moment of rest, which does not last — by swallowing a few marvels, I undertake to refute them from within.

One of these legends, which merits my credulity for at least one short dance, sets men without heads strolling about on the beaches of the newfound islands, those islands situated behind the horizon where Olivier Maillard's Franciscans are drawing plans for their future churches. In that land, there would exist some of those acephalous creatures, with straight shoulders, and the sulky bearing of thickset men: I dream of having a chance to stroll over the beaches of fine sand and gold, good for the hourglass; I dream of camping for an entire season alongside these creatures with their truncated busts, from which no stalks rise nor any heads tremble. Neither for them nor to me is acephalism an infirmity, as it does not bar walking, nor does it impede gesture, nor does it prohibit man from using his arms or his two hands and, in consequence of a convenient arrangement, it implies neither deafness nor blindness. The singular disadvantage of acephalism, passing sometimes for an advantage, would be that it precludes having a face, and the whole range of expressions that go along with it: in fact, headless man is deprived of manœuvres used in the season of love & at councils, he cannot worry himself over a wig, nor about his moustache, however much it might be confused with such hairs as are found on our chests. The acephale is a poor courtier, incapable of that gymnastics practiced by palace-goers, incapable of mastering even on his chest the art of smiling or of disdain, without which there can be not only no politics, but also no language. We will not see acephales at the royal courts, those in which, at this very instant, are striding discoverers, mapmakers, prelates, projects for the new world, and proprietors to whom fences are dear. We will not see them haunting the antechambers in the role of confidants, because it is inconceivable to think of a Catholic queen leaning over the belly of one of these monsters to share a State secret. If they frequent the palaces, these acephales will play the role of lackeys with great competence, or be bailiffs, and we will feel we can speak in perfect frankness in their presence, as freely as before a bronze bust. On the other hand, the acephale escapes the judges, because they cannot put a face on the criminal, nor order his decapitation; for all of these reasons, the acephale strikes me as mostly agreeable; I know not whether this sort of amity might prove reciprocal.

Far from brainless, the acephale only lacks a cranium, which absence spares him several times a year the conversation of barbers and hairdressers. He is still capable of thought, and all its functions and its virtues, even better disposed to them as his thought does not come in contact with the cold found in the interior of a head pierced by seven holes, rather, it is a thought more deeply and more secretly situated, betwixt the heart and the stomach, seats of unvented love and anger; in that place, thought is a slow combustion, not some variety of sneezing.

Acephales do not wear hats, a more noticeable anomaly on our soils than on those legendary islands where, rain or shine, most of the natives go about nude, but represent their modesty, according to certain missionary brothers, with some twine, wrapped front to back. Acephales have the rustic manner of the most fatigue-stricken peasants, those whom the use of a plough sets straight, their entire bearing is that of common labourers, which bearing the weak intellectual, vitiated, pale and suffering from so many sensitivities, interprets as a sign of honesty. The loves of the acephale are somewhat violent and voracious; as soon as the first kisses are given the embrace is consummated, nothing or very little separating the preliminaries from rape; and, if our literature of love is to be found between those intervals, then courtship is an art absent from the world of the acephale. On the basis of realism, the missionaries, soldiers for the pope, complained of these monsters, complained to see all our sermons, my own included, fly right over these creatures without even touching them, the reason for this being, their conscience: they have insulted these acephales impervious to eloquent speeches for so long now that I would prefer them as my peers.

Acephales lead bitter lives if they cannot give or receive a kiss, they are morose companions if they cannot drink without sullying the spout, and, since their ears can never be found, no one entrusts to them any false rumour.

According to their *rarissimes* letters, which refute one another, the navigators would have found Atlantis out there half-emerged, the island of the Cynocephales, the home of men with a single eye in the center of their foreheads; it were as if all of our sprites and bedtime stories have been led off to that land, in that ocean where the waters of the Atlantic mix with those of the sea of China. If all the creatures in our bestiaries have taken refuge there, in order to freshen up or to play at distances, if every improbable country is there, then why should we be content with only the island of the Cyclopes and why not also discover the kingdom of Torelore there in the same vicinity, where custom mandates that it is the man who is to stay in bed while the wife gives birth? Why should we be content to situate the Amazons there, and not also the country of Cockaigne too, which the *Trionfo dei poltroni* so justly describes? And since we are told that a great many natives at the other end of the Ocean eat human flesh, prepared with no more than a bit of seasoning, one last humanity in the very midst of depravity, nothing bars us from thinking that the headless anthropophagi of the country of Blemmyæ are hiding there too, whom Pliny describes in his vast inventory of things. We know that the explorers went ashore in those precincts at the Invisible Isles, and at the Hidden Isles, and at the isles designated as Useless, surely also at the Fortunate Isles evoked ages ago by Cicero, and surely they climbed up on that smooth, white dome which is the giant egg of the bird of Roc Island; will they at last see off in the distance, rising up out of the fog, the summits of the Mountain of the Virtuous Wife, where a woman waited so long for her husband to return that she was changed to stone, as the wives here are increasingly doing? Eventually they will reach the very ordinary shores of Camphor Island; for their salvation and for our sake too, they will make a conquest of Melita Island, where bushes in the shape of humans climb around in trees in order to embrace them, and also a conquest of Lixus Island covered with the tree that bears golden fruit; they will go ashore without much difficulty at the volcanic Pyrallis Island, the Isle of Ambergris and the Isles of King Mihrage, where sea-stallions go to breed; and seeing how nothing is free to remain any longer in the secrecy of our imaginations, or in the pages of books, they will bring down to the earth, with the help of flags, swords, decrees, acts of annexation *& Inter Cœtera* bulls, those lands heretofore suspended in midair, like the City of the Apes and the magic castle of Yspaddadenpenkawr, which seems to withdraw at precisely the rate at which one draws near.

We will have to resign ourselves to the idea that to berth is the common lot of man, together with the long-distance voyages of our day, so long as they bring us back spice and gold (likewise, we must resign ourselves to the idea that in times of war — and I would not know how to say where they begin, where they end — circumspection is mistaken for stupor, the first words of a rebuttal for surrender). Of course, the new world is a mirror for gulls, or the gulls in the mirror, or the reflections of the sun on a piece of cut glass, but, in the absence of a new world, our sailors & ship-holders, whether genuine or false, will go on finding useless islands elsewhere, to set up their trading posts. The day that every tribe will have been uprooted, the day it will no longer be possible to go on inventing new lands to exile our unwanted mercenaries to, the day we will no more be able to pretend to mistake an Ottoman for an Indian, the colonists so frustrated for victims, for want of natives abroad, will at last colonize their very selves.

Which is to say: we will finally colonize ourselves, we will look ourselves up and down, and find ourselves picturesque — our own innocence will bring tears to our eyes, we will want to observe ourselves naked, and we will marvel at our shamelessness, if it is of the same kind as Adam's; we will act as pedagogues towards ourselves, we will be thorough, irritated at times by our nonchalant or infantile appearances, and our ineptness when it comes time to decipher the legal texts whilst droning them out, the decree of Gratian and its innumerable commentaries; we will abandon ourselves to a death by starvation since our reason admits of hunger as cause and death for consequence; we will study our own deaths as curious, measurable events, to be taken down and notarized by clerks of justice, compassionate priests, men in charge of the parish registers; we will feel a scathing pity on our behalf; we will save ourselves from ourselves in little groups, in enclaves, & we will be astonished to see ourselves survive — then we will inflict the Gospel upon ourselves and, in view of the ever-growing number of crimes we perpetrate against ourselves, we will encourage the rite of forgiveness, and make forgetting the condition of universal beatitude; we will be curious, not just about ourselves and the tribe to which we belong, but about our most minute particulars, and we will care to know only of our foibles and our ridiculousness, the wading bird's crest raised in mating season; we will want to know nothing of ourselves but what is known of vanished civilisations, to have but a fibula as the proof of our existence, a fragment of a vase, fragments of stories, a single, sublime cantata, just one, and the remnants of funerary rites. (Finally, we will entrust the memory of humanity to a few librarians, because they are the ones who are eliminated the most rapidly, with the approbation of the laughing onlookers; then we will look in vain for our name in books, and this will be yet another form of eternity.)

I see it now: the worst that could befall us would be to be discovered by bearded adventurers (ourselves), descending from caravels at once familiar and perplexing — that is to say, to be subjugated, invaded, treated as incompetents, as if we were idiots or children, incapables sold by slave merchants, bought up by priests, adored like rare minerals or totems once it has been proven the god they represent never existed, neither on earth, nor in heaven, nor in some perpetual conflagration. For my part, I hope that this comes to pass: that foreigners, strangers to Eve and Adam alike, before coming ashore or instead of doing so, will invent us, and grant us this concession: attribute treasures to us and grant us intentions which we will never understand, then consider our swine as fauns and our lepers as cherubim, our wounds as ruby-coloured ornaments. The best that could happen to our continent would be to be invented, just as today, even as these pages draw down to their end, the fomenters of the new world are inventing archipelagœs in the form of crescent moons, and daily bringing us back some more jewels, one more indigene yet (more lucky finds). It would only be fair: to have our turn to be invented by so many untold, intrepid, impatient, gullible strangers, well-versed in real or imaginary geography and the use of the arquebus, wily and imaginative men with strong appetites (all possible appetites), fools with an imagination to prevail over hunger; to be invented by a coalition of clerks, of poets and merchants, of popes and sovereigns, of painters and mercenaries who worship Igraine; to be invented by cabinets of men unable to check their phantasist tendencies or even their small sense of humour, and their sense of the absurd, now and then the sense of the grotesque. Short of forming the objects of a razzia, it is our right and perhaps our need to be invented by energumens, lovers of nest-eggs and calligraphy, amateurs of caricature and old legends, of books of chivalry, readers of Lucian, Fournival, Merlin, and Ariosto, men who go off without a care in the world to hunt down the Snark or the Hippogriff, especially if they do not exist (because that leads them to formulate still deeper burrows, and uses of camouflage they have yet to master) — dreamful men greedy for gain, yet sensitive to the nuances of a story and of psychology, as the caliph in the *Arabian Nights* was to the uses of ellipses. Wrongfully they will take our continent for an Eldorado or the gates of paradise, and they will be keen to act out their adventure novels on our old world soil, which will have the benefit of enchanting our deserts. Would heaven that their oblique readings nourish the idea they form of us: then will we essay to resemble their imagination, if we find it to our liking and if it figures us as pacifists, ingenious and handsome. I look forward to the day when they will say that we walk about on streets of silver, that we have the heads of birds, that our wives' blouses conceal golden apples; because, to accept to go on living on this continent grown grey and agèd in a single night, such strangers, hypothetical but quite alive, would have to vouchsafe to our land and our people all that we have bequeathed to the so-called new world: sundry images, sundry names, sundry fruits, sundry centaurs and unicorns, sundry mountains of gold, sundry diamond mines, sundry navels in the form of emeralds, sundry spectres, sundry forests, sundry palm trees, sundry rejuvenations at the fountain's spout. Now to wait for a ship sailing under the two-tone flag of generosity and avarice to dock on our shores, only to depose at our feet these riches belonging to no one — to no one.

Afterword

On the Peregrinations of Vâtsyâyana

The facts can be reconstituted as such (it is however impossible to be both concise & thorough): in London, in 1883, 250 copies were published of a 198-page *in-octavo* with the exact title *The Kama Sutra of Vatsyayana, Translated from the Sanscrit, Complete in Seven Parts, with Preface, Introduction and Concluding Remarks. Benares: Printed for The Hindoo Kama Shastra Society* — to which the editor adds: *For Private Circulation Only*. The most interesting thing here, with regard to our present purposes, is certainly not this *For Private Circulation Only*, nor even the fact that the famous Hindoo Kama Shastra Society, absent from all official directories, certainly never existed (no more so than the Cythera where *The Education of Laura* was printed) — the most interesting is how, in the middle of a 19th century agog for Orientalist facts and fictions, trinkets and truth conflated, a Brahmin sage aided by some erudite Englishmen succeeded in producing a correct edition — as correct as possible under the circumstances — of the *Kāma Sūtra* of Vâtsyâyana, which was at the time on the brink of being lost to humanity forever. The details of this labour are given in the *Catena Librorum Tacendorum* ("on curious and uncommon books"), edited by Pisanus Fraxi and *privately printed* in London, as well: one article relates the tribulations of the pandit Bhugwuntlal Indraji (an honorary member of the verifiably real Royal Asiatic Society) during his attempts to locate a passage of several pages discussing the art of biting.

Just imagine: this famous Indian erotic treatise, henceforth available in every format and in the most various forms, even the worst, was then on the brink of being lost to oblivion, of rotting away in the dark and humid vaults of some library (the Westerners first heard of it by chance: while reading the *Anunga Runga — The Stage of Love* — in which there are recurrent allusions to a certain Vâtsyâ, about whom nothing more is known, except that his real name was Mallinago or Mrillana). In Bombay, the last remaining copy of the *Kāma Sūtra* was incomplete and in a deplorable state; to put the fragments back together, Bhugwuntlal Indraji set out to obtain copies from Djaypour, Benares, and Calcutta that were likewise damaged and incomplete (because if pseudo-Vâtsyâ's treatise is authoritative by its presence in the catalogue of every library worthy of the name, it was hardly possible in the time of Bhugwuntlal the pandit "to obtain the integral text" — I quote from the introduction to the English edition). Thus, a comparative reading & meticulous cross-referencing of the five or six lacunary copies permitted a more or less respectable (at any rate recognized as such) text to be established, and appreciated by erudite Londoners, those of *private circulation*, for whom Sanskrit would remain an eternal enigma.

However, cross-referencing alone would not have sufficed: because, as stated in the *Catena Librorum Tacendorum*, the original, or rather its various copies, were composed in a Sanskrit that was both obsolete and obscure, "difficult to decipher in certain places," Bhugwuntlal the pandit, spurred on by these Englishmen enamoured of the Orient and the art of engraving, was inspired to make use of a providential *Commentary* on the *Kāma Sūtra*, "copied from the library of the king of kings Vishahdava." An ironic twist of fate well known to philologists: a large part of Vâtsyâ's treatise thus found asylum in its *Commentary* and remained concealed therein, just as the immense *De Natura* of Heraclitus was incorporated over the centuries into the books of Musonius Rufus and of Pseudo-Plutarch, who cite it in passing, almost with casualness, without realizing how lightly they play with time and with oblivion, & with memory.

Elements of Bibliography

Even if it does not go the way of the Silk Road, the text of the *Refutatio major*, attributed to Antonio de Guevara, is subject to the same desuetude, the same intermittencies, the same periods of dormancy during which its pages are effaced & its language lost — before other accidental rescues, other chance rediscoveries. And like Vâtsyâ's erotic treatise, the *Refutation* of Anthony would require us to weave together six or seven fraudulent copies, six or seven paraphrases, and several commentaries, even petulant, in order to reestablish the text in its entirety.

AFTERWORD

In our day, all that we can do is to take out from the Pamplona library three loose pages, in Latin, kept together in a folder (pages probably dating from the 18th century). Arezzo is more fortunate, for its library possesses a *Libro di Marco Aurelio con l'horologio de' prencipi: distinto in 4 volumil composto per Antonio di Guevara*, published in Venice in 1575 by Francesco Portonaris: an Italian version containing, after the book of the emperor Aurelius, a *Grande Confutazione*, which is nearly complete. The Bibliothèque Nationale in Paris has a *Refutatio major* in Latin, dating from the end of the 17th century; but anonymous, fragmentary, and in a piteous state (many pages are missing, including the title page). The library of Lisbon contains a *Libro llamado Menosprecio de corte y Alabança de Alvea*, attributed to *Don Ant. Gevara*, in three languages, Latin, French, Spanish: the final section of the volume contains the text of the *Refutation* in an inspired Spanish translation, often fantastical (but it cuts off two-thirds of the way through). *Horologium Principum, sive de vita M. Aurelii, ab Antonio de Guevara* (Henningus Grosius, 1632) can be found in the Library of Grenoble with the shelf mark C 4853: by far the most reliable extant version, but still imperfect (*Refutatio major* runs from pages 697 to 783; unlike the copies in Arezzo and in Lisbon, this version includes neither the dedicatory epistle, nor the pæan to Pope Joan, among other lacunæ).

The text presented here relies essentially on the Grosius edition; it was however necessary to consult the Venetian (Francesco Portonaris) & Lisboner copies in order to fill in several lacunae and reestablish (confirm where necessary) some of the more doubtful readings (apropos of Luther, it is indeed a question of *lard* — *lardum* — and not *Lares*; as for Peter Martyr d'Anghiera, he is not three feet tall — *tripedalis* — but he trembles or he stamps — *trepido, trepide, trepidare* — et cetera). In most instances, the versions proposed by those who, over the centuries, cited the *Refutation*, sometimes fecklessly, have not been retained — except in a few exceptional cases (the saying: *so long as the calendar convinces us of the existence of tomorrow, instead of complaining, the lenders tally up their interests*, comes directly from the *Cosmographia Universalis*: in those two lines, Sebastian Münster summarizes what Guevara had developed over fifteen).

Until now, there existed no modern edition of the *Major Refutation*, with or without an author's name, with or without corrections; the most recently available edition is that published in Lisbon (*Libro llamada...*), dated 1782: if the *Refutatio*, in its early years, elicited the admiration of respectable authors (a form of knighting), it later gave rise only to curiosity, and over the years amusement, becoming a collector's item for Wünderkammer enthusiasts (or specialists of books and of rare quotations: compilers with the airs of stud farmers). On certain occasions, when the clerks feel a sudden craving for the unadulterated truth, it will send them back to the memory of the slayers of received ideas: freethinkers of the Thomasius or John Toland type, so easy to excite.

AFTERWORD

Myths, Emblems, Clues

It is generally agreed that between the Lisbon edition of 1782 and the allusion to the *Refutation* made by Fernando de Alva in 1891 (*Obras Historica*), just over a century of total silence elapses during which the *Refutation* becomes neither an object of study nor the subject of mockeries, nor a curio to be displayed in a cabinet alongside a chunk of amber: but nothing, truly nothing, the equivalent of all those ghosts printed in minuscule characters which fill our libraries up to the ceiling (and which inspired Thomas De Quincey's sense of vertigo). The amateurs of Oriental erotism had plucked Vâtsyâ's name out of the pages of a treatise on love entitled *Anunga Runga*; today, the curious reader of the *Refutation* may find Guevara's name, his life, and his work in one of the chapters of *Wooden Eyes*, signed Carlo Ginzburg — a historian famous for having attended the witches' sabbath and likening the world to a spoilt cheese. He evokes Antonio, the pseudo Marcus Aurelius, the *Horloge des princes*, and the lousy character of Marcolphe — not a word, however, of the *Refutation*: whoever wishes to go down that road and satisfy a conspiracy theorist's curiosity should consult footnote 67 of the book *Clues, Myths, and the Historical Method*, by the same Ginzburg: it tersely invites researchers to find "all the forms of creative abductions in the *Grande Réfutation* of the pseudo Antoine de Guévare" (sic).

Still hot on the trail of Guevara (pseudo-Guevara or real Guevara) the honest and curious man will consult the indexes and the libraries (in an ordinary index, *Guignol* is found just before *Guillaume II*): and this is how he will find a reference to him in the *Christophe Colomb* of Soledad Estorach and Michel Lequenne (1962 — going against what is commonly accepted, the authors affirm that admiral Columbus discovered America "because he was searching for it"). He will also find him in note 4 of the first chapter of volume 2 of Braudel's *Méditerranée*. He will learn that Marguerite van Berchem, in September 1953, in a text entitled *Sedrata, une ville du Moyen Âge ensevelie sous les sables du Sahara algérien*, cites the *Refutation*, as does Enrique de Gandi, in 1929, in his *Historia critica de los mitos de la conquista americana*, and William Horgaard in 1914 in *The Voyages of the Norsemen to America*, published in New York — and that is just about all.

Reconstitution

According to the most likely scenario, Antonio de Guevara, confessor to Charles but not yet Bishop of Guadix, writes his refutation in absolute secrecy in 1525. At the time it is an open letter destined to a circle of friends, but very soon the text leaks out, passing clandestinely from clerk to clerk, from consul to consul in diplomatic pouches; the bookseller-printers of Italy (they themselves design the fonts, we should recall, with which they will spread the word), the editors and their young assistants speak of the *Refutation*, we can imagine, in hushed tones while shaking their heads, as we in our time might speak of a romance soon to be tried in court.

The rumour reaches the prelates, probably even the pope (it was then Clement VII, and he believes not a word of it); someone translates the Latin text into the vernacular and eventually a small circle of bank brokers finds out about it; soon several printed versions are circulating, the presentation quite variable, the editorial conventions not yet solidified. (Twenty years prior, a copy of Amerigo Vespucci's *Letter to Lorenzo de Medici* is dispatched to Paris from Lisbon, a certain Fra Jocondo takes it upon himself to translate it into the church Latin of the day, and in a short while fourteen Latin editions of this text, henceforth entitled *Mundus Novus*, are brought out all over Europe, along with ten or so versions in vernacular languages; from 1507 onwards, which is to say three years after Amerigo's fourth voyage, his *Mundus Novus* is incorporated into the *Pæsi Novamente retrovati* printed at Vicenza. The *Letter to Soderini* by the same Vespucci meets an almost identical fate: printed in Florence in 1505 by Piero Paccini, it gets translated into French from a manuscript copy, then translated into Latin and published in 1507 in the *Cosmographiæ Introductio* under the title *Quattuor Navigationes*, before being finally translated into German in 1509, that is to say printed in Gothic: which makes the text formidable and in a way inaccessible, like the idea of a chain-mail vest.)

For a long time, the *Refutatio* circulates without an author's name, and this is how many booksellers, humanists, cardinals and retired navigators first hear of it and come to refer to it: it crops up in a letter of Antonio Pigafetta, in the *Description of Africa* of Leo Africanus, published in 1550 but composed around 1526, in the *Tratado sobre las justas causas de la guerra contra los indios* (1541) of Juan Ginés de Sepúlveda. After the publication of *The Dial of Princes*, the tongues seems to loosen up a bit & authors are less hesitant to attribute the hard-to-obtain refutation to Antonio de Guevara, henceforth raised to the rank of bishop: for example Rui Faleiro does so, in 1535, in the *Tratado de la Esphera y del arte del marear*. From roughly the 1550s onwards, a little before or after, the uncritical & seemingly undisparaging attribution to Guevara starts to take on the weight of evidence for some authors, or rather of custom, in the same way that the *Song of Songs* is without fail ascribed to Solomon and *The Book of Revelation* to John. Guevara's identity acquires its solidity and triumphs from this fixation, but by the same token it is reduced to so little: a household name, subject to the strange apotheosis of antonomasia (sic). Alvar Núñez Cabeza de Vaca, as well as Francisco Ávila, in *Trattado y relación de los errores, falsos dioses y otras supersticiones*, in 1598, & José de Acosta in his *Historia natural y moral de las Indias*, and many years later John Eliot (1647) in the *Essay to Bring the Indian languages into Rules*, finally Robert Burton himself will speak without hesitation, but also without reflection, of the *Refutation-of-Guevara*.

Major Attribution: Antonio de Guevara

We are naturally distrustful of evidence, especially when it reaches unanimity, or nearly does, which is a form of beatitude, prior to canonization (because in his testament Christopher

Columbus claims to have first seen the light of day in the sweet city of Genoa, many historians are inclined to disbelieve his every word: they seek to join, how humanly, that club of scoffers and idlers who can never be fooled). The bores will bicker amongst themselves, the sly ones will keep at their embellishments, a great many names will be cited: nevertheless, the most serious candidate, not the most picturesque one I admit, remains Guevara, such that the best will be saved for last, to wit, two serious contenders for the title, proposed by Bartholomæus Keckermann and Alonso Fernández de Avellaneda: respectively, Amerigo Vespucci himself, and Joanna, the Queen of Spain, called *La Loca*, The Mad, who died in captivity in her convent at Tordesillas.

Let us consider our Guevara first: although he is not sulphurous like Pomponazzi the atheist, nor Luciferian like Pietro Bembo, the church satyr, he proves himself elsewhere capable of facetiæ & even of imposture: capable for example of composing a manuscript (full of adages and anecdotes), attributing it to the emperor Marcus Aurelius, claiming to be its translator or simple depositary, then divulging some choice excerpts under that inoffensive conceit to a certain number of friends. We know how scornfully the English philologist Meric Casaubon regarded Guevara's imposture, as we also know the lapidary judgement expressed by Pierre Bayle in his *Dictionnaire* (usually more nuanced: but this good old Bayle could not resist the pleasure of turning down a bishop at so cheap a cost): neither of which prevented pseudo-Marcus's pseudo-book from enjoying an immense success.

AFTERWORD

Among the evidence incriminating Anthony de Guevara: that natural or artificial skill of counterfeiting in the era of *l'arte del disegno*, the vogue for heteronymy and the inevitably transparent masks of the written word, to which we should add, the numerous similarities between the figure of Goat-Hair-Miles (present in *The Dial of Princes*) and that of Esau (in the Lisboner version of the *Refutation*). Miles is a barbarian, *as hairy as a bear, his spear in hand*, who travels from the far side of the Danube to the Senate in Rome to give a speech to the waxy and manicured Romans in the style of Tacitus (*Agricola*: the diatribe of Calgacus, chief of the Caledonians, before the imperial troops: *you made a desert, and you call that peace*). In the Lisbon *Refutation*, Esau is invoked as the patron saint of the countless poor commoners who are taken advantage of by clever cadets. The one and the other have *a small face, intense eyes, a tanned complexion, coarse hair*, they wear shoes of porcupine leather: we might call that a coincidence, but the author of the *Refutation* himself preferred relations of causality to simple coincidences by far. (Specialists require just seventeen similarities between fingerprints to root out a suspect.)

To establish a connexion between the *Refutatio major* and *The Dial of Princes*, graphologists would have to compare the curves of the s's and the crosses of the t's; Lorenzo Valla for his part would have compared the respective styles & spoken of syntax: but it is difficult to compare a fantastical Latin, a Latin of the church or of the court, warped by idioms, to the Spanish of a native speaker translated into sixteenth-century French or English. The fact remains, though, that the Guevara of *The Dial* (the Guevara of the *Book of Marcus*) shows a great facility in the pamphlet style, not least by preterition, a glibness one would hardly expect in a confessor, even if he was raised on prebaroque Spanish (which is to say schooled in immoderation, in the folly of faith and of cape-and-sword combats, in barking contests that pit scholastic Latin against mystical Latin, the *Sentences* of Peter Lombard against *romanceros* — contests which later, much later, would culminate in Quevedo's torrents of obscenity and the great feats of valour accomplished by Quixote). Obviously one has to hear Guevara's voice to have an informed and thus an accurate opinion of it; for want of anything better, here is the translated version (Miles, the peasant who has come from the newly conquered territories, is addressing the members of the Senate in an ambiance of togas and scrolls): *Look closely at what you have done, for the gods have no duty towards it, nor men to finish it, nor the world to complete it, or the world would not be the world, or fortune would drive in the nail, or what has never before been seen would be seen, and what you have gained in eight hundred years, you would lose in eight days, for nothing could be more just, since you have made tyrants of yourselves by force, than for the gods to make slaves of you in return.* Or this: *Would that you know, if you do not, that when the poor people go before the triumphant chariots, saying, Live, Long live invincible Rome, elsewhere the poor captives are saying in their hearts, Justice, Justice.* Or again: *I do not know what folly betook Rome to go off and conquer Germany, because if lust for its treasures was the cause, without comparison more money was spent on its conquest and presently is being spent to defend it, than all our rents from Germany combined [...], and it may perhaps be that we will lose it before we will have recouped what it cost to conquer it.* And lastly: *I have seen things being done in this Senate that if the least of them were done on the banks of the Danube, the gallows would be more thick with thieves than the vines with grapes.*

First Minor Attribution: Amerigo Vespucci

Whoever apprehends Guevara would as soon think he had his culprit — but in the last years of the sixteenth century Bartholomæus Keckermann (in *Systema theologiae* he affirms: "Hell is certainly somewhere, though to give its precise location may be impossible" — and in *Apparatus Practicus* he voices the idea that one only travels abroad in order to boast about it) claims to have proved contrary to common sense that the author of the *Refutation* is Amerigo Vespucci, the adventurer-for-hire of the Medicis. (*Contrary to common sense*: death having suddenly swept Vespucci away in 1512, with the haste with which blunders are swept over. In Keckermann's view, a shrewd bank calculator, capable of usurping the great explorers, of securing the title of *pilote major de la casa de contratación* for himself, of hiring an office of scribes to write a letter to Lorenzo di Medici, of antedating his discoveries, and of adding his first name to the freshest of world maps, Vespucci would not have had any scruples about choosing, to best suit his gallantry and his needs, the date of his death, as well as the circumstances.) (Vespucci, dead in 1512? the detective novel taught us to remain suspicious in the presence of a dead body, especially if by the cadaver's side there kneels a widow, and between the two a widow's pension of 10,000 maravedís a year — life insurance frauds have a distant precursor here: as a matter of fact, Vespucci was so poor in 1512 that he was ready to die six deaths in six different principalities, in order to receive six pensions from six princes, payable in cash.)

However fraudulent it might appear, this hypothesis merits our full consideration: for it has the advantage of examining more closely the situation of a figure usually taken for granted: all we know of him is that he was a young man who profited from circumstance — the spirit of the age — and a single portrait of his face, in the *Cosmographiæ Introductio*. Vespucci is generally made out to be a bank employee, a virtuous missionary a notch brighter than the rest, an agent one sends off to the provinces to settle disputes, or a confidence man accorded every liberty so long as all the gold pieces are accounted for. He is a son from a good family, but a ruined family in the service of the Medicis, possessing neither their gold nor their art; he passes most of the time for an honest man, not excessively cultured (he would cede less readily than others to the eternal temptation of mannerism), sufficiently scrupulous to have the silver in the coffers entrusted to him, but capable on the loading docks of hoodwinking his audience at the last minute, by a trick of accounting. There you have the standard portrait (which the *Refutation* itself belies);

Bartholomæus Keckermann prefers to situate Vespucci under the aegis of Mercury, for a set of reasons that would add up to a biography if they were laid end to end. By imitating the professorial, scholarly lunacy of Saussure, by declaring himself a disciple of the audacities and cunning of Michæl Servetus, Keckermann demonstrates that the name *Amerigo* is none other than a bastardized Florentine form of *Mercurio*: and if by this name Vespucci is not the reincarnation of Hermes, stranded in Florence, he would be one of his sectaries, more or less in secret, more or less boastful, playing off dissimulation and publicity, with bravado.

Mercurian Amerigo, according to Keckermann (to sum up the *Apparatus Practicus*): a swift, flighty being, loquacious, plurivocal, polyglot, trading with men of letters, rhetoricizing with merchants, playing the lute whilst accompanying himself on the abacus which he plays like a pair of maracas or a cymbalo, it depends. A man of voyages, always on the go, ever elsewhere: but different than the Cortéses and the Columbuses: because, while they set off on adventures, Amerigo is happy to just slip away, the essential thing being not where he is headed, but the place he leaves behind.

Vespucci is mercurian because he proves himself a poet, he plays with words to the point of dropping his name into the atlas, as he would leave his fortune behind on a desert island (it will be transformed, over time, into a fixture of the pirate novel: coffer, portolano, manuscript, gold nuggets), he appreciates the nuances of a yard of fabric and is spontaneously awestruck before the paintings of Piero di Cosimo (the serpent of La Simonetta) — his artistic, sometimes dandyish tenderness does not prevent him from appreciating the finer points of trade, as a game of numbers and a quotidian Kabbalah, as an invitation to the voyage or as the miserable status quo in the era of humanism.

The assimilation of Amerigo to Mercury is an approximative shifting of letters, it might be no more than that, we could close up the book like a music-box, to let a meditative, doubt-ridden silence resume its hold. But Keckermann does not stop there: he argues, he proves that these mercurian auspices make Vespucci virtually a godsend, that his sharpest sense before sight (eyes like a hawk) or hearing (perfect pitch: the inimitable G-sharp of Venetian ducats) is his nose for opportunity: Mercury or Hermes, it's the fruit that falls from the tree and the lazy sleeper's luck that matter, a beautiful precision, being under just the right branch. According to the *Apparatus Practicus*, that opportunism explains how, without lifting so much as a finger, one can manage to claim someone else's voyage for oneself (a printer in Holland once published the travelogues of a certain Balthasar Sprenger by simply replacing every instance of his name with that of Vespucci).

Vespucci is not content to just give America his first name (ensuring that *by chance* his letters reach the workshop at Saint-Dié-des-Vosges), but publishes within only a few years of each other a description of the New World and its systematic refutation. To affirm both A and not-A, so as to be right at any cost and cover the immense field of possibilities:

in the eyes of a mercurian, that is a godly sport, inaccessible to mortals but that's not all: Vespucci, bard of commerce and of the stock exchange, knows that in every human enterprise subject to shifts of fortune the most basic precaution consists of investing in at least two sectors simultaneously. *Quattuor navigationes* and *Refutatio major* are not the symptoms of a divided spirit, they are the mark of the soundest common sense — some of his contemporaries, in Florence & elsewhere, would see there an accountant's shrewdness.

Little does the course of events matter, the destiny of the world, optimism or pessimism, decadence or Paradise, the end of time as a poorly built raft or as the eternity of island sands (the opposite of lassitude): Amerigo Vespucci, as they say, wins on both counts.

Second Minor Attribution: Joanna

No two ways about it: impossible to know what mischievous scholar hides behind the pseudonym of Alonso Fernández de Avellaneda, the few documents available in Tordesillas, his native city, have only set the historians wandering back & forth between León and Castile. With or without a face (arbitrarily, I grant him that of Quevedo), Avellaneda tried to become famous by publishing three short works under this assumed name: the first, in 1614, hopes to capitalize on the fashion of the day for Quixotism, but its humour is only lukewarm; the second, a mixture of verse and prose from around 1623, is an homage to Lady Pretext, she whom young Dante interposed between his gaze and his one true love Beatrice (a profile in the style of Filippo Lippi) to fool the observers (white Guelphs and black Guelphs at High Mass). The last book (*El libro de los días en cualquier parte del mundo*) is dedicated to Tordesillas, its royal palace, its monastery in the Mudéjar style; from chapter four onward, Alonso valiantly seizes Joanna the Mad, cloistered in her castle there, like a lover ravishing his fiancée under the eye of her uncles. For Avellaneda, the queen mother, known as *La Loca*, no more insane than Charles V or Henry VIII at the same time, is the true author of the *Refutation*: a letter from a usurped ruler addressed to her usurper.

Avellaneda's hypothesis (Joanna defrauded, thrust aside and set up in an asylum by King Charles and his Flemish eminences, so to leave the throne empty for the taking) resumes some of the arguments the *comuneros* put forth at the time of their revolt: to restore The Mad would be to oust the king. For Alonso Fernández as for the insurgents of 1520, it's no question of madness: just a touch of that melancholy to which great men are prone, here justified by mourning, excessive faith, and the weight of responsibilities. It would have taken some shrewdness, on Charles's part (his councillors: a menagerie of baboons who mill around the palaces, making and unmaking reputations), to translate her being blue into outright madness: the confinement at Tordesillas is a coup d'état, no less, Charles rules over an empire, stretching from Antwerp to Eldorado, Joanna receives a fief of twelve square meters, heated by a stove, visited by a confessor.

Her mind is going? that is what the ambassadors have been persuaded to believe: they suppose an idiot lying prostrate on a tile floor in Tordesillas, hardly stirring save on Sundays, when some kind souls conduct her to mass (then the visage of Philip the Handsome comes to be superimposed on that of the Savior: the aquiline nose and raspberry lips). Officially, it is harder to make the queen disappear in her capacity as queen, & for a long time Joanna's name will continue to be seen at the bottom of royal proclamations, followed only by that of Charles — it will take some time for this protocol to fall into obsolescence, as if it were an old Castilian custom. By disappearing (writes Avellaneda), Joanna cedes her place to the modern world (which is not quite accurate).

Aphasia as Dignity

Charles arranges the confinement, a donjon, a convent, a cloistered cell, as though that ceremony brought the official period of mourning to a close; he lets it be known that behind a locked door Joanna's madness becomes extravagant, conversant with demons, she tears out her hair one by one to offer to posterity a smooth, ring-wormed head, screams at the full moon, incapable of the least attention to practical matters. However, Joanna's madness, independent of Charles's posturings, might be of an altogether different order, not given to the hysterics of Medea, but obedient to the rule of mutism, of reflection, of immobility, of reading and of writing, searching in the play of shadows for ghosts in the form of hypotheses. Avellaneda insists on this point: the madness of Joanna is reason's last sovereignty — following the example of Sor Juana Inés de la Cruz: we must use our intelligence to our benefit.

The prostration of Joanna, after the death of her husband, Philip the Handsome? a critique of funerary protocol and of the ensemble of signs conceded to the living by the gods of the pantheon — puerile variations on disgust and reification. In that case, the solitude of Joanna and her mutism would be the severity of a strong-willed woman facing up to the casualness of the facts, of our ceremonies, and facing up to the amateurism of the Church, as it happens: when death, despair, and the metaphysics of the void are at the door, only mediocre stuccadors and well-combed priests come to our aid. To remain unyielding, and circumspect, that is the only form of mourning available to a woman who, by virtue of her rank, accedes necessarily to the spiritual dimension of all things, and would not know how to content herself with mundanity (much as it is in the nature of certain dandies, heirs of Ruskin, to derive an entire æsthetic from the most ordinary of objects). No lamentations over the coffin, no kissing of the death mask, no dirges or crying fits, no metaphysical guignols à la Edgar Allan Poe.

To Charles or to the beggars whose liberty is defined by the length of their chains, to the courtiers free to move about inside the courts, the reclusion of Joanna appears as a capital punishment or an admission of her own invalidity; at the time of the great discoveries, the Madwoman assigned to such a small & precisely delineated part of Spain functions as the still point around which all the world turns & each measures their progress: whether it be a question of climbing the social ladder or of land manœuvres. For others, the reclusion of Joanna, which she perfects by remaining silent, is the certainty of her all-powerfulness, a relinquishment of the signs of authority to others less fortunate, who lack that certainty. The sole lunacy of Joanna then consists in locating the navel of the world (held to be in Jerusalem by a few puzzleheads) halfway between her bed & her writing desk, or in the middle of her own body — in other words, the axle of the universe turning.

Over many pages the valiant Alonso de Avellaneda defends his simple idea: the silence of Joanna the Mad is the silence of a defendant sure of her right before a presiding judge. Her mutism is her answer to the politics of her adversary as deployed in speeches, in letters, in ultimatums, indebted to the rhetoric of Rome, incapable of shutting its mouth. (A mutism so radical that it leads the prison guards to forget the meaning of silence, to lose its sense as speech and view it as just the first symptom of resignation: her mutism must have been a scathing reply to the strategies of language, become, as so frequently, the final treasure of the vanquished and an unmistakable form of surrender: in the eyes of her guards.) The intelligence of Joanna takes a vow of silence: because speaking amounts to being conscripted into the grammar of the enemy, he who has just triumphed — the time to speak, then, will be when every figure of style will elude her adversaries, even if that means having to speak Hebrew, or Nahuatl. Not too dissimilarly there are stories brought back from America of monkeys who chose to keep silent to avoid being taken as slaves.

Her madness is the proclamation of the truth ("I am the Queen of Spain") from the depths of a labyrinth built on (and guarantor of) illegitimacy: Joanna becomes a heroine with neither voice nor fame, who could nonetheless have shared a table with Bruno and with Galileo, or even with Jesus were he better company, or with any other adventurer for Truth in the land of fools; for centuries now her name has been invoked by persecuted minorities in search of references. However, screaming at the usurper from the depths of one's gaol is in itself hardly sufficient to warrant being called insane (especially seeing as the madness of Joanna was defined as mute: faithful to silence as Mozart was to the timbre of the clarinet): it is more judicious to calmly compare the logic of Joanna's legitimacy to the logic of Caroline legitimacy: a job for the experts, quarrels for the jurists, the byzantine iota in the sole brainpan of the old lady selling pippin apples.

The hebetude of Joanna, feigned or real: to decree, in the perimeter of her cell, that the true laws of the empire will hold sway there, and the dynastic order, the true one, be respected: mad everywhere else, Joanna is sovereign in her cell, and of this at least, she is perfectly conscious.

AFTERWORD

Joanna the Mad, Author of the Refutation

We might have guessed: a woman of Joanna's heart is ill-suited to a room measuring just three by four meters: the daughter of Isabella, she is a creature who does not abdicate without a struggle — the army of her son is solid, but despite all the precautions her Castilian stubbornness makes it impossible for her to go on living like a plant among shadows. To avoid having to hear her scream bloody murder out the embrasure (which she probably would never have dared), her captors offer her a reasonable quantity of pens, paper, and ink in compensation for the loss of her freedom. Joanna *La Loca* takes advantage of her enforced idleness and scores of pages (from the paper vendors of Leiria) to write *canzones* and *romanceros* in the style of Sebastián de Córdoba, who inspired John of the Cross; later, not by much, she dedicates herself to writing prose, in the mode of the elegies and works of religious devotion which she read over and over when she was not imitating the *Amadis de Gaul,* as Teresa of Avila will later do, it seems, at Carmel. Presumably she works on her memoirs: her childhood in the chancelleries, her union with Philip, son of Maximilian, her wedding night, her passion, her jealousy, her bottomless love for this prince handsome as an archangel of Mantegna, which is to say as the Eros of Apuleius, but encumbered with the weapons and armour of a knight, which weigh him down. She would have described that archangel, and his death and the breakdown it precipitated, the panic and fear she felt, and how she cursed the god of her ancestors *&* his damned twists of fate;

she would have confessed how through the long night she held a cadaver in her arms, not to cling to the little life still remaining (an odour of lard), but rather to absurdly try to comprehend death, its eventuality, & the meaning of this comedy. After having exactingly evoked the corrupt body, the lamentations and the affronts, the cortèges so long that they stretched across all of Spain, she was unable to prevent herself from following her husband's mortal remains beyond the gravestone into the depths of the Earth, and without leaving his side for an instant adventuring through those spaces rife with shadow and incessant griefs which constitute the abode of the dead. To perpetuate her love, to perpetuate Philip himself, perhaps also to conserve what still remained of her sanity, Joanna took it upon herself to describe the beyond as precisely as possible: its extent, its depths, its entrance situated within the crater of Etna, its vestibules and its guardians. Seeing that the land of the dead exists down to its smallest details, no uncertainty will stop her when, driven on by chagrin or the sentiment of injustice, she would travel there to retrieve Philip the Handsome (Avellaneda, or Joanna, seems to forget that during his lifetime, Philip did everything in his power to oust his wife: like a stuffed doll).

Joanna-according-to-Avellaneda has an eloquent pen, which does not stop when on such a roll: in this land of the dead vast as a crypt and rife with pandemonium in its lowest depths, she is not content to lay to rest Philip the Handsome, a pale blue statue, but she also, like Dante, consigns to that domain all those who were living up until quite recently on the surface of the Earth: sycophants from Toledo, Grandees from Spain, and monks from Castile; she makes an especial effort to enrol in her hell those persons who disappeared overnight, whom Charles, and Isabella before him, dispatched to the American Indies to get them out of the picture. There remains in the *Refutation* a trace of these hells in the form of a Spanish inn, an asylum for those undesirables the court condemns to exile. According to Avellaneda, Joanna knew that Emperor Charles would read these pages & ultimately decide their fate (the fire of the hearth or the waters of the Guadalquivir?): it is surely to him that she addresses this farcical danse macabre, where all these enemies come together in a Tartar atmosphere enlivened by some light music: to feast, to discuss the times which pass, and to go on living, so brazenly.

The abode of the dead: quite simply the place where each of us goes, where all things terminate: from that morass Joanna fishes out those whom Charles drowned & who drowned on the voyages of discovery, she fishes out the sacrificed sailors and the fake natives, the Jews sailing on the wide open sea, the fabulators in the emperor's employ, the Vivaldi brothers who vanished in the west, the shipmates of Magellan who saw the inverse of the sky, one of the Pinzón brothers who died of syphilis in the care of quack healers and who, some hours before his death, resembled so little one's idea of a man.

General Gonzalo de Córdoba, exiled by Ferdinand, was able to endure his solitude only by staying abreast of the latest court news — how, then, does Joanna the Mad, in her nun's cloister, stay up to date on all the latest rumours, on subjects as varied as headless men living on the beaches of Brazil, the devaluation of the florin, and the intrigues of Peter Martyr d'Anghiera? Despite her limitations, she receives (according to Avellaneda) visits from distant cousins who remain loyal to the queen mother (minor nobility: handsome, old-fashioned types come to regain their lost prestige through contact with the Mad), she presides over her salon, so to speak, welcoming to her bedside colonists who come back ruined from Hispaniola, just as she agreed to receive a delegation of discontents, at the height of the *Comunidades* crisis. She listens to their grievances, pretends to take them into account (a smooth demagogue beneath her neurasthenic front); all the country's fleeced shareholders and empty-handed sailors come to her bedside table to offer an unforgiving portrait of the New World — Joanna is content to just lend an ear, but what an ear she lends.

If the queen decides to send her work back to oblivion, all she needs to do is confide it to King Charles, care of her jailer-confessor; if on the contrary she wishes to give the text a small chance of survival, a ruse becomes necessary: Avellaneda suggests that Joanna lets her book trickle out page by page, in the form of friendly letters addressed to cousins in Saragossa, priests on post in Pamplona, her former chambermaids and other convent sisters, brides of Jesus Christ, near Lisbon, austere laundresses. But how so many loose pages scattered over fifty million acres could have been assembled into a single book, that is something we will probably never know.

AFTERWORD

Other Candidates Considered

All facts considered, the chances are slim that Vespucci would have written a *Refutatio major*, even if on numerous accounts he does appear sly and even if he was one of the few, in his day, to know about the portrait of Simonetta by Piero di Cosimo. There is no question that he died in 1512 and that, despite the carnivalesque ghosts wandering about between worlds and manifesting themselves to naive believers, Amerigo was already long returned to dust the day someone penned the first words of the Epistle to King Charles V — (the paragraphs consecrated to Vespucci himself seem not to bother Bartholomæus Keckermann: he considers that self-portrait the height of mannerism in the era of Pontormo and of the *Self-portrait in a Convex Mirror* by Francesco il Parmigianino). Joanna the Mad's luck is just as bad: a recluse, starving herself, certainly a mute, she would not have been able to compete with the renowned prodigality of Sor Juana Inés de la Cruz. Whatever one says of it, the news coming from the West Indies when it reached the door of her prison must have sounded to her ears like the fables of Esplandián, full of golden armour, but it is rather improbable that Joanna would have had enough strength to build an argument around it — she probably passed her long hours knitting, awaiting the return of the caravels.

Amerigo and Joanna abandon us, one falls into paludism, the other grows gaunt in her madness, neither being so lucky to disappear into the horizon; they leave us in the sole company of Guevara, the crotchety bishop and voluble confessor: not the most cheerful of companions. We'll get used to him though: the attribution of the *Refutation* to Father Antonio has long been accepted more on the basis of tradition than pertinence (every author may stand on the shoulders of his predecessor, but a return to the source has never been the same as finding the original: his personal archives were empty, we know, of any concrete proof, just as Rome, according to Guevara, was in the time of Marcus Aurelius "devoid of any man who would dare speak the truth").

Either what is already a given (to speak of Guevara's *Refutation* as one speaks of the *Requiem* of Mozart or the *Adagio* of Albinoni, or even of the *Kreutzer Sonata*), or doubt and the game of attributions: which are variations as delectable as cream puffs (or the moment of hesitation before cream puffs). If we decide to forgo the figure of Guevara (a bishop? a confessor and a giver of lessons? just an old beard), if we decide that Guevara is a name as hollow and enigmatic as that of Pseudo-Dionysius the Areopagite, then we can permit ourselves the pleasure of drawing on the list of suspicious authors, active between 1500 & 1530, who lack a serious alibi. And fortunately the list is long, since it is an era of antitheses & controversies, an era of graphomaniacs, omnipotent, omnivorous savants, compilers, encyclopædists, curious men and bibliophiles: whoever wants to enumerate them all must have a steady voice and lungs of steel. For Conrad Gessner (*Bibliotheca Universalis*), the author of the *Refutation* is Laonikos Chalkokondyles, a Greek polyglot who (according to Burton) attributed Babylonian customs to the English; for Guillaume Postel (*De Orbis terræ concordia*), it is Pope Pius IV; according to Pierre Bayle (*Pensées sur la Comète*, 1680), one would have to look rather in the direction of Willibald Pirckheimer, senator of Charles V and geographer, who never left his bed, owing to attacks of gout; according to Athanasius Kircher (an erudite and sometimes absurd Jesuit, inventor of the magic lantern and failed decoder of hieroglyphics), Leo the Hebrew is the man, and for Sor Juana Inés de la Cruz, who is clearly mistaken, the author is Athanasius Kircher; Thomas Browne (*Pseudodoxia Epidemica*) proposes the name of Ludovico Ricchieri, according to whom the Gorgon was none other than a woman of stupefying beauty; John Toland, *champion of the truth* according to his own epitaph, claims in *The Origin and Force of Prejudices* that Pietro Bembo is the man, that cardinal who refused to marry his mistress Faustina so that he could keep receiving his ecclesiastical benefices (at the same time he appears to have been carrying on a platonic relationship with Lucrezia Borgia); for Giambattista Vico (*Scienza Nova*), it's Johannes Trithemius, who invented the word *steganographia* (before dying around 1516); for Balthasar Bekker (his *The World Bewitched* argues that devils are in truth but wicked men, and angels but virtuous ones), it is a certain Lilio, canon at the Archbasilica of St. John Lateran and the last stalwart defender of the world's flatness; for Christian Thomasius, it is Gregor Reisch, who in the *Margarita Philosophica* of 1503 makes the southern hemisphere out to be an immense ocean; finally, for Saint-

Évremond (he did not wish to pass up a chance to speak), the author of the *Major Refutation* can be none other than Pietro Pomponazzi, the Paduan, according to whom miracles are a product of the human imagination (*De naturalium effectuum admirandorum causis seu de incantationibus liber*, 1556). (To attribute the *Refutation* to Garci Rodríguez de Montalvo, author of the *Amadis* and *The Exploits of Esplandián*, was an idea that occurred to no one — a shame, really: one reads in *Esplandián* the name of California, the first appearance of the word, thirty years before its discovery in 1542.)

Rubrics from Lorenzo Valla

Lorenzo Valla (*Discourse on the Forgery of the Alleged Donation of Constantine*) demonstrates that the *Decretals* are a poorly executed forgery by a minor ninth-century clerk (wrongly, Isidore of Seville was suspected), not only because it is nearly impossible to imagine Emperor Constantine I giving all of Rome, no less, to little Pope Sylvester as though it were a quill, but also because the document itself is full of "contradictions, impossibilities, stupidities, barbarisms, and absurdities." Whosoever would wish to have the pleasure (exquisite paleographer's pleasure) of refuting the *Refutation* could make use of the same tools, and place under the rubric of *Contradictions*: the phrase *wax with age*, in the epistle dedicatory, applied to King Charles when he was only twenty-five years old.

Under the rubric *Impossibilities*: the allusion to the works of Fracastoro, published only in 1530, and the occurrence of the word *cyanide* (*curare* in the Arezzo version, a Caribbean word meaning: *when it comes, we fall*). Under the rubric of *Stupidities*: what the abbot Boileau would have termed an abundance of nude throats, since in the *Refutation* are to be found more naked girls than in a thousand pages of Las Casas, or in the New World itself even. Still under the rubric of *Stupidities*, the plural accorded to the very unique Martin Waldseemüller, and to the recycling of an old commonplace: the image of the Barbarian heroically refusing the joys of the Christian paradise. Under the rubric of *Idiocies*: the excess of conjunctions, a fantastical punctuation (and not always faithful to its own fantasies), Gongorisms incompatible with the rigor of argument, a propensity to slide like a fare-dodger from the literal to the figural, which is the mark of unsure litigants.

Lorenzo Valla reproached the author of the *Donation* (whose last name was Palea or Palea Ecclesiasticus) for writing *luminariorum* instead of *luminarium* and *concubitores* (bedmates) instead of *contubernales* (roommates); I for my part reproach pseudo-Guevara for writing *simia* instead of *simila* (finest wheat flour), *quantuluscumque* instead of *quantumcumque*, and instead of *esculuntus* (edible) preferring *osculabundus* (giving kisses). Finally, under the heading of *Absurdities*, it would suffice to point out that a confessor, a "bishop of Guadix then of Mondoñedo," would certainly not give confused accounts of stories in the Bible, and would not use the names of Spain and Castile interchangeably with such casualness.

(Moreover, it would have been difficult for Joanna to affirm that she never knew Isabella, or that she frequented the doctors of Padua — that is, unless a band of psychiatrists were brought by force all the way to Tordesillas.)

Conjecture as Odyssey

Pietro Bembo, Johannes Trithemius, Gregor Reisch, Vespucci so far from his America, Queen Joanna so far from her sanity, they all escape us, by going their separate ways; they seem to be following the steps of a danse macabre (which rounds up entire populations and claims to reveal the meaning of life), but a frivolous dance as at a marriage (the marriage of no one in particular: dancing just to dance). To be sure, none of them (Antonio de Guevara included) seem to worry themselves much about the *Major Refutation*, and still less about its attribution; they would gladly leave us alone with our uncertainty and our clues, leaving behind them, without remorse, a pile of pages as volatile as ash.

The common joke Lutherans make about papists (that joke taking the place of argument): given the number of relics in the patrimony of the Roman church, one would seriously have to consider the existence of a six-armed St. Matthew, & a twelve-footed St. Francis. The text of the *Refutation* permits us to catch fleeting glimpses of an Antonio de Guevara with neither head nor bust: the *Major Refutation* would be the book of an author who did not write it; the paradox seems impassable, but not as much so as that of the Holy Trinity, much less so than the dogma of Mary Theotokos.

AFTERWORD

The name of the author matters little, the game of attributions is more entertaining than an irrefutable authority, especially if hesitation is involved, of a less sad sort than the usual — to the point that attribution, a job normally reserved to the archivists (those of the *Künstlerlexikon*), becomes a genre to rival the chivalric romances. In scholarly works, which strive to award this or that *Madonna with Crayfish* to this or that painter, since all things assume their legends and since rumours are taken seriously, the miracle of the author's transformation into a character is made complete.

Coda

In 1897, Samuel Butler propounds the theory that Homer was in actuality a woman from Sicily; a few centuries earlier, Giambattista Vico had furnished the proofs for the non-existence of Homer, and advanced the audacious hypothesis of a community of authors confused with the community writ large. In turn, Francis Bacon and Alphonse Allais will cast doubt on the existence of William Shakespeare: Bacon substituting himself; Alphone Allais (less vain but more conscious of the great enigmas of the world) substituting a nobody named "William Shakespeare." Richard Whately publishes his *Doutes historiques* in 1819, Jean-Baptiste Pérès his *Grand erratum, source d'un nombre infini d'errata* in 1827: together the two usher in a long line of historians determined to prove either that Napoleon never existed, or that he is still alive (Pérès and Whately belong in the former category). Around 1900, Pierre Loüys proposes that Corneille is the sole author of the plays of Molière, and in roughly the same epoch Ferdinand de Sausurre demonstrates that all ancient Roman poetry was, in all truth, constructed according to an alphabetical system as rigorous as it was secret. The tradition seems to nearly bottom out when in 1941 Rex Stout demonstrates in *The Saturday Review of Literature* that Doctor Watson is a woman, and Sherlock Holmes a village halfwit. Bolder still, in our day, German academics demonstrate with the cleverness characteristic of the genre (its richness the result of attention to minutiæ) that Pope Sylvester II & Emperor Otto III invented the years separating 614 from 911 outright, the Emperor Charlemagne in his long fur robes being a product of their imagination. Finally, let it be noted that Erik the Red, in a saga from the twelfth century, attributes the discovery of America to Leif Erikson, & not to Barni Herjólfsson, whose existence he refutes.

COLOPHON

THE MAJOR REFUTATION
was handset in InDesign CC.

The text & page numbers are set in *Adobe Jenson Pro*.
The titles are set in *Fell Duble Pica Pro*.

Book design & typesetting: Alessandro Segalini
Cover design: Sergio Aquindo & Alessandro Segalini

THE MAJOR REFUTATION
is published by Contra Mundum Press.
Its printer has received Chain of Custody certification from:
The Forest Stewardship Council,
The Programme for the Endorsement of Forest Certification,
& The Sustainable Forestry Initiative.

Contra Mundum Press   New York · London · Melbourne

CONTRA MUNDUM PRESS

Dedicated to the value & the indispensable importance of the individual voice, to works that test the boundaries of thought & experience.

The primary aim of Contra Mundum is to publish translations of writers who in their use of form and style are *à rebours*, or who deviate significantly from more programmatic & spurious forms of experimentation. Such writing attests to the volatile nature of modernism. Our preference is for works that have not yet been translated into English, are out of print, or are poorly translated, for writers whose thinking & æsthetics are in opposition to timely or mainstream currents of thought, value systems, or moralities. We also reprint obscure and out-of-print works we consider significant but which have been forgotten, neglected, or overshadowed.

There are many works of fundamental significance to *Weltliteratur* (& *Weltkultur*) that still remain in relative oblivion, works that alter and disrupt standard circuits of thought — these warrant being encountered by the world at large. It is our aim to render them more visible.

For the complete list of forthcoming publications, please visit our website. To be added to our mailing list, send your name and email address to: info@contramundum.net

Contra Mundum Press
P.O. Box 1326
New York, NY 10276
USA

OTHER CONTRA MUNDUM PRESS TITLES

Gilgamesh
Ghérasim Luca, *Self-Shadowing Prey*
Rainer J. Hanshe, *The Abdication*
Walter Jackson Bate, *Negative Capability*
Miklós Szentkuthy, *Marginalia on Casanova*
Fernando Pessoa, *Philosophical Essays*
Elio Petri, *Writings on Cinema & Life*
Friedrich Nietzsche, *The Greek Music Drama*
Richard Foreman, *Plays with Films*
Louis-Auguste Blanqui, *Eternity by the Stars*
Miklós Szentkuthy, *Towards the One & Only Metaphor*
Josef Winkler, *When the Time Comes*
William Wordsworth, *Fragments*
Josef Winkler, *Natura Morta*
Fernando Pessoa, *The Transformation Book*
Emilio Villa, *The Selected Poetry of Emilio Villa*
Robert Kelly, *A Voice Full of Cities*
Pier Paolo Pasolini, *The Divine Mimesis*
Miklós Szentkuthy, *Prae, Vol. 1*
Federico Fellini, *Making a Film*
Robert Musil, *Thought Flights*
Sándor Tar, *Our Street*
Lorand Gaspar, *Earth Absolute*
Josef Winkler, *The Graveyard of Bitter Oranges*
Ferit Edgü, *Noone*
Jean-Jacques Rousseau, *Narcissus*
Ahmad Shamlu, *Born Upon the Dark Spear*
Jean-Luc Godard, *Phrases*
Otto Dix, *Letters, Vol. 1*
Maura Del Serra, *Ladder of Oaths*

SOME FORTHCOMING TITLES

Hugo Ball, *Letters*
Carmelo Bene, *Our Lady of the Turks & Other Texts*

ABOUT THE TRANSLATOR

Jacob Siefring, MLIS, MA, studied French literature
at the Université de Nantes & at McGill University.